12 Conversations with

American Studies Scholars

12 Conversations with

American Studies Scholars

Leslie Wilson

P R E S S
A M E R I C A N A

Hollywood • Los Angeles

Press Americana

http://www.americanpopularculture.com

12 conversations with American studies scholars / edited by Leslie
Wilson.
pages cm
ISBN 978-0-9829558-0-2
1. College teachers--United States--Interviews. 2. United States--
Civilization. 3. United States--Civilization--Study and teaching. 4.
College teachers--United States--Biography. I. Wilson, Leslie, 1967-
editor of compilation, interviewer. II. Title: Twelve conversations
with American studies scholars.
E169.1 .A1113 2015
973.0092'2--dc23
2015001155

TABLE OF CONTENTS

NANCY BENTLEY

Professor Nancy Bentley holds a Ph.D. in American literature and culture from Harvard University and chairs the Department of English at the University of Pennsylvania. She has published two books: *Frantic Panoramas: American Literature and Mass Culture 1870-1920* (University of Pennsylvania Press, 2009) and *The Ethnography of Manners* (Cambridge University Press, 1995 and 2007). She is also the co-author of Volume Three of the *Cambridge History of American Literature* as well as the Bedford Cultural Edition of Charles Chesnutt's *The Marrow of Tradition*. She serves on the Editorial Board of *PMLA*, *ALH*, and *Nineteenth-Century Literature*; has received fellowships from Yale, Penn, Dartmouth, and Boston University; and has been honored with the Lindback Award for Distinguished Teaching.

I asked her about her second book, *Frantic Panoramas*.

What attracted you to the topic of literature and mass culture at the turn of the twentieth century?

In retrospect, I think my interest was sparked by current discussions about the crisis in the humanities. Literature scholars have been grappling with the digital revolution. Do long novels and centuries-old poems still matter in the age of the internet? In our image-saturated world, are the textual worlds created in *Moby-Dick* or *To the Lighthouse* obsolete? At a certain point, I realized that the anxieties and euphoria fueling these discussions (are digital media tapping unforeseen human capacities? Are they damaging our ability to think and feel deeply?) were uncannily familiar.

1

I knew from earlier research that there was the same sense of crisis a hundred years ago, when the advent of mass culture – dime novels, early cinema, tabloid papers, mass entertainment – made for a similar kind of cultural disorientation. Media scholars talk about the "industrialization of communication" in the late nineteenth century and show how it upended virtually every domain of public discourse. I came to see the mass culture of this period as kind of prehistory to our own digital era, and I wanted to explore what that history suggests for the value of literature and literary study.

I think the history I tell may hold clues to our own crisis as humanists – some of them discouraging but others quite hopeful. I'm convinced that humanities disciplines have unique capacities for understanding the current media revolution and its global effects. Literature in the traditional sense is now at the margins of public culture, but literary analysis – modes of thinking that are not just numerical but historical and critical – remains a powerful kind of disciplinary thought. And a relevant one, too – perhaps now more than ever.

What inspired you to write *Frantic Panoramas*?

The germ was a paper I wrote about car crashes in the fiction of Edith Wharton. Wharton almost never included sensational plot turns or catastrophes in her novels; the sledding accident in *Ethan Frome* is the closest she comes to making a story hinge on an irruption of literal violence. But I noticed that, throughout her fiction she returns again and again to the *metaphor* of the train wreck or car crash. In some novels, the trope appears up to four or five different times. It began to seem like a tic, a kind of compulsion. Why this recurrence to such an unlikely image? I found it doubly intriguing because Wharton was writing her novels at precisely the moment

2

when the early filmmakers discovered the glamour of cinematic crashes. The head-on collision of two trains, the dynamite blast of a wall, the wreck of an automobile or a barn wall – these and other crash scenes were among the earliest short films in cinema, and they were an instant hit with filmgoers. Interestingly, Wharton herself despised movies. She thought they pandered to a lowbrow taste for sheer sensation, and she declared that radio and cinema were "two worldwide enemies of the imagination." What could it mean, then, that she relied on the same cinematic energies of speed, risk, and violence to tell stories about the social lives of rich people?

This puzzle prompted me to think about how some of the authors often written off as "genteel" or culturally conservative – Wharton, Henry James, William Dean Howells, and Henry Adams among others – had actually imported into a highbrow literature much of the same "aesthetics of astonishment" (as one film scholar has dubbed it) that you could find in cinema and the popular press. Scholars already recognized that African-American writers like W.E.B DuBois had combined a refined literary style with an aesthetics attuned to the violence of modernity; what of the similar conjunctions discernable in the work of other literary intellectuals in this era like Adams or James?

I was intrigued by this convergence of opposites; it seemed like a compelling thread I could follow to see where it would lead. My hunch was that this sensationalist aesthetics could help me tell a different kind of cultural history. I became less satisfied with the standard explanation that said this era was the beginning of a "great divide" between high culture and mass entertainment. I wanted instead to think about the way both literary writers and mass culture producers were obsessed with very unliterary energies: velocity, shock, novelty sensations, and spectacles, and what Henry James called "the imagination of disaster." Eventually, I became convinced that writers' encounters with mass media and culture – hostile though they often were – in fact allowed for an acute literary analysis of new kinds of experience and meaning in modernity.

Explain the "high literary culture" and its "self-appointed task of analyzing mass culture." Why was this so?

It's long been known that more elite writers looked on with dismay as mass fiction, tabloid newspapers, and advertising began to dominate the culture. But I became intrigued at how often writers expressed an almost visceral sense of bewilderment at this change, as if experiencing a kind of vertigo. One editor confessed that "at the mere sight of a row of paperbacks, I am conscious of a feeling of nausea." Howells said he experienced "impossible stress from the Sunday newspaper with its scare-headings, and artfully-wrought sensations." For Wharton, viewing close-up shots in movies was akin to having a suffocating "nightmare."

In short, the same novel sensations and heart-racing topics that delighted popular audiences produced something closer to queasy panic for these literary writers. But this wasn't because these intellectuals were simply too fastidious to enjoy these novelties. It was something more fundamental. They recognized that the world of letters was no longer the foundation for the public sphere. Since at least the eighteenth century, the shared tastes and habits of mind cultivated by a literary education had defined public reason and governed public debates. But suddenly the authority of letters was clearly eroding. Jürgen Habermas and others have shown how the late nineteenth century was in effect the twilight of the world of letters, the beginning of a "postliterary" age. Profit-driven publicity had far more influence than cultural criticism. Mass opinion mattered more than reflective deliberation. Howells complained that literature had become just one more product in the entertainment market: "if you don't amuse your reader, practically, you cease to exist."

To be sure, then, there was a new divide between literary culture and mass culture. Literature and art had become more cerebral and reflective – realist painters and writers were dubbed "the analytic school," for instance – while mass culture ushered in new sorts of sensational experience, from amusement park thrills to the zany chases of Keystone Kops. At the same time, however, writers did more than just lament this state of affairs; they also turned their analytic gaze on this dizzying new media environment. I think we have largely missed the way writers were able to *combine* analytic thought and the unruly sensory experience they found in mass culture. So in *Frantic Panoramas*, I reposition literary writers not as mere reactionaries but as the first media theorists – the first intellectuals to try to think through the implications of the industrialization of print and image.

Edith Wharton and Henry James figure prominently in your study.

Both writers were Europhiles. Both were intellectuals and believed that highbrow literary traditions carried a kind of cultural authority that was being eroded by mass culture. But these same facts also made them highly curious and critically alert to the way mass media and commercial culture were transforming everything – language and letters, taste, even subjectivity. James (quoting the word recently coined by French intellectuals) distilled these transformations as the function of "'modernity,' with its terrible power of working its will." This disposition made them critics of modernity in a

5

double sense: they were critical of its "terrible power," but they were astute observers of both the possibilities and risks that power entailed. (Their Europhilia, however, also made them blind to much of what modern imperial power was doing around the globe.)

Wharton, as I have suggested, was keenly attuned to the changes in human subjectivity brought on by the new speeds and shocks of modernity. People first began noticing these changes with the advent of railway travel. For the first time, passengers were subjected to a stream of intense stimuli: unpredictable low-level shocks, the whizzing by of objects in one's field of vision, a constant awareness of physical risk. These physiological changes created what historians call an "industrialized consciousness" – a new kind of mental orientation to the world, and one that spreads throughout populations as agricultural societies become "risk societies."

Wharton was skeptical and more than a little anxious about these changes. In her mind, they were degrading the more reflective sensibilities concentrated in literature and high culture. The characters she skewers most savagely are usually those addicted to high-speed travel and mindless stimulation; for the vapid nouveau riche, she writes, "life whizzed on with a deafening rattle and roar." It's not surprising, then, that the first industrial art form, cinema, struck her as akin to an obscenity of overstimulation, a bombardment of the senses. As Walter Benjamin observed, cinema was the first art form to make shock a formal principle of artistic production. At the same time, though, Wharton's discomfort with the conditions of an emergent "risk society" is also the basis of a searing social critique. She knew that modern risk, while by definition a matter of chance, is not distributed evenly. In her fiction, the greatest damage from modernity falls on two particular groups: vulnerable women and neglected children – those

6

who, even within the most affluent classes, are the most expendable, the most easily cut off from the protections of wealth and position.

So Wharton knew the distribution of risk is not random but socially patterned. And she captures the social vulnerability of figures like Lily Bart in *The House of Mirth* by describing her as living always on the verge of a "possible crash." Today we have the almost bureaucratic phrase of populations "at risk"; Wharton began tracing fault-lines in modern risk almost a century ago. And she did so by drawing on stylized figures of violent accidents and potential crashes that filmmakers were exploring as well. In this way, she anticipates the long line of novelists who developed a "crash culture" aesthetics, from Fitzgerald (an admirer of Wharton who has the working-class woman killed by a speeding car in *The Great Gatsby*) to J.G. Ballard (whose erotic dystopia *Crash* features marginalized characters seeking sexual gratification through observing or experiencing car wrecks). I find it striking that in the last decade or so, a brand of social critique like Wharton's and early cinema's infatuation with violent accidents have come together in films like David Cronenberg's adaptation of Ballard's *Crash* and the Paul Haggis movie of the same name that won an Academy Award.

For his part, Henry James was most fixated on the popular press: the tabloid papers and the "flood of books" produced for mass sale. James complained that US culture, unlike Europe, was dominated by the commercial imperative of publicity – the constant push to display, to sell, and to court the masses. He linked this "pestilent modern fashion of publicity" with mass education and what he called America's "newspapered democracy." So there was certainly an anti-populist strain to his fixation. He admitted to feeling "lettered anguish" at these changes.

At the same time, however, his lament about commercial publicity has other dimensions to it. He recognized what Jürgen Habermas, a leftist, has described as "the disintegration of the public in the sphere of letters" that occurred in this period. This was a process whereby market-driven publicity began to crowd out the kind of public discussions and reasoned debates conducted in "high literacy" publications. Long before Habermas, then, James worried about the way the mass press could manipulate public opinion for private ends. The "mechanical reverberation" of war lust in the press troubled him in particular. (Sounds familiar, no?). And he realized that the omnivorous nature of publicity ("publicity as a condition, as a doom") was dissolving the boundary between high art and popular culture, thus putting literary value up for grabs. Once writers, readers, and presses conspired to make literature a mere "article of commerce," there is no way to define the literary as such. As he put it, "all this depends on what we take it into our heads to *call* literature."

And yet this same insight – that, finally, literature is simply whatever we call literature – also gave James a measure of hope. It certainly gave him a far-reaching sense of what the future of literature might turn out to be. He wrote a fantastic essay called "The Question of the Opportunities" in which he meditated on how mass culture, for all that it was destroying, was also sure to offer new *kinds* of literary value, new sorts of cultural forms and communities. He grasped, for instance, that the public sphere was becoming less like a single open forum and more like a chessboard, with many different "publics" created from different sorts of appeal and access. And he also anticipated that, given such "colossal" mass production, the sheer volume would give rise to exciting new kinds of art that would burst through narrow rules and restrictive conventions. In that sense, James predicted both the achievements of high modernism and our current explosion of new media.

I can mention two examples where this forward-looking side of James emerges in his own work. One of his lesser known novellas, *In The Cage*, is a story about a young working-class telegraph operator in London. His interest in this figure anticipates the genre of "railroad thrillers" in early cinema, such as *The Grit of the Girl Telegrapher* and D.W. Griffith's *The Lonedale Operator*. After being kept outside of public discourse, women were suddenly insiders; literally, they had their finger on the switch. While filmmakers exploited this fact to display a beautiful young woman's "grit" in a crisis, James's telegrapher turns out to have an extraordinary talent for interpreting coded social messages. She manages to decipher – and eventually, to become a participant in – the covert communication between a pair of aristocratic lovers. The story shows James's fascination with the way mass media had the capacity for creating new languages and social relations.

Another example of James's openness is his interest in the place of Native American life. In his remarkable book *The American Scene*, he speculates at key moments about what modern America must look like to the Natives displaced by railroads and cities. But, even more significantly, he describes an encounter he had with "a trio of Indian braves" touring Washington, D.C. What strikes him most is the way these men are *not* the Indians represented in literature; as he puts it, they defy "a mind fed betimes on the Leatherstocking Tales." They are instead fully present subjects of modern history. They wear bowler hats and carry tobacco and photographs like countless other Washington visitors. For James, the closest comparison is not Cooper's Indians but "Japanese celebrities," an analogy that suggests images from the mass press. These Indians have survived the "bloody footsteps of

9

history" and stride boldly on what James calls the "printless pavements of the state." In this moment, then, he shares the same fascination with the sight of Indians that made Geronimo an international celebrity. But here James uses mass culture iconicity to try to grasp the present and future place of Native Americans in their long, vexed relation to the U.S. state. Literary history has to be jettisoned while mass culture offers him resources.

Were there any surprises during your research and writing?

From the first, I knew I would examine the role of race; early popular forms like minstrelsy and plays about Indians provided the DNA, as it were, for American mass culture. But I was surprised to discover the very complicated, dynamic relationship that Native- and African-American intellectuals of this time had to mass culture.

Bastions of high culture like the American Academy of the Arts, which was founded during this period, excluded people of color (and blackballed white women for a long time as well). High culture was white culture. And yet this was still a time of great innovation for native and black intellectuals. In 1897, a group of writers and educators founded the American Negro Academy, attracting leading figures such as DuBois and poet Paul Laurence Dunbar to join this scholarly society. Some years later, a group of Native-American writers and activists founded the Society of American Indians, the first pan-Indian organization to publish journals and hold conferences.

These writers were just as wary of mass culture as people like Wharton and James – more so, in some respects, since they saw far more keenly how mass entertainment often fed on

10

dehumanizing racist stereotypes. At the same time, however, they also saw commercial culture in a different light than their white counterparts. They knew that, because artists and actors of color were excluded from the mainstream, lowbrow entertainment such as musical theater and early cinema were among the only places that African American and Indian performers and artists could pursue their work. As a result, these intellectuals recognized that commercial culture – for all its racist energies – was still a sector that was far more open to the innovative styles of black and Indian writers and performers than the literary establishment was.

I was fascinated to learn that Dunbar, the first black American poet of real renown, had written musicals with all-black casts for the off-Broadway stage in New York. One of his productions toured the country in 1898 and set off an international dance craze. Similarly, the writer James Weldon Johnson gave up his career as an educator and lawyer to write plays for black musical theater. Both writers won recognition from the white establishment for their literary works; but they still found that these early forms of mass culture – popular music and dance – allowed for the kind of innovation and creativity bubbling up from what Johnson called "Negro bohemia" or urban street life. Like the emergence of jazz in this period, Dunbar's novel *The Sport of the Gods* and Johnson's *Autobiography of an Ex-Colored Man* are fueled by the unruly, wildly creative energies of working-class black life that was beginning to find expression in mass culture.

In a similar vein, a number of Native-American intellectuals from this period saw Wild West shows and early cinema as venues that offered a chance for cultural expression and even the possibility for political agency. The writer Luther Standing Bear complained loudly about the way many early filmmakers produced distorted portraits of Native-American

11

life. But he didn't reject the medium of film itself. Indeed, after his early career as a star in Bill Cody's Wild West show, he performed in Hollywood westerns alongside actors like Douglas Fairbanks, and he served as a consultant for Hollywood producer Thomas Ince. Charles Eastman, another Native-American writer who was also a founder of the Society of American Indians, took the same position: he saw Indian shows and westerns as "a new line of defense of native Americans."

How did the book affect your teaching?

During the time I was researching *Frantic Panoramas*, I taught some graduate seminars that addressed these topics. In designing the seminars, it was easy to select theoretical and historical studies that allowed us to put mass culture in a scholarly context. But I wanted the students to have some first-hand experience searching the archives for their own discoveries. So I invited students to do some digging for little known materials pertaining to turn-of-the-century mass culture.

The results were fascinating. One student discovered a magician from the West Indies who was popular among black American audiences and was featured in one of the first magazines published in the black press, *The Colored American Magazine*. Others pursued some of the more obscure corners of the Chicago World's Fair or the archives of early film. In a few cases, I asked the students if I could incorporate their discoveries – fully credited, of course – in the book. In that sense, my students affected the book as much as the book affected my teaching.

RAY B. BROWNE

Professor Ray B. Browne founded the *Journal of Popular Culture* and the Popular Culture Library at Bowling Green State University in 1967, the Center for the Study of Popular Culture at BGSU in 1968, the BGSU Popular Press and the Popular Culture Association in 1970, the Department of Popular Culture at BGSU in 1972, along with the *Journal of American Culture* and the American Culture Association in 1978. He penned almost a thousand book reviews, published about two hundred articles, and wrote or edited over sixty books, one of the most notable of which is his 1988 history about the battle to establish popular culture as a legitimate field of study, *Against Academia.*

Clearly, popular culture studies would not be where it is today – if it would even exist at all – without the contributions of this important scholar. He even provided us with our most thorough and lasting definition of popular culture: "Popular culture is the way of life in which and by which most people in any society live. In a democracy like the United States, it is the voice of the people – their likes and dislikes – that form the lifeblood of daily existence, of a way of life. Popular culture is the voice of democracy, democracy speaking and acting, the seedbed in which democracy grows. Popular culture democratizes society and makes democracy truly democratic. It is the everyday world around us: the mass media, entertainments, and diversions. It is our heroes, icons, rituals, everyday actions, psychology, and religion — our total life picture. It is the way of living we inherit, practice and modify as we please, and how we do it. It is the dreams we dream while asleep."

13

I asked him about his struggle to legitimize the study of popular culture.

We know you began in folklore. What first attracted you to the formal study of everyday life?

I have always had a great deal of hope for the possible accomplishments of human intelligence if properly used, and to me so-called "higher education" was the route to that accomplishment. But I have thought that this "higher education" meant teaching the mind to think, not necessarily to remember. In other words, thinking was more important than remembering.

Growing up in Alabama, I looked over at the University of Alabama – and other colleges – and thought I saw that there was a great field of everyday life that needed to be studied and understood. From 1947 to 1950 I taught at the University of Nebraska, famous for the folklorist Louise Pound, who had just retired, and my deep feeling for the importance of folklore was strengthened.

Tell me about your time at UCLA. Isn't that where you first formed this idea of studying something called "popular culture"?

After three years of teaching at Nebraska, I went on for a Ph.D. at UCLA. There my feeling about the importance of the study of everyday culture was strengthened – or perhaps allowed – by two of my professors, Wayland Hand, folklorist, and Leon Howard, an important scholar in American literature. Wayland did not understand what I was talking about when I told him I wanted to study "popular culture," that is everyday culture as distinguished from folklore (though

14

they are essentially the same, except in different media). Leon Howard understood what I was talking about and allowed me to go ahead, especially after doing a summer's collecting of folksongs in Alabama. I told him about collecting The Lord's Prayer as a folksong. He thought that was significant.

Why is the study of popular culture important?

For a civilization to flourish and continue, it is important that all aspects be known because up until recently they were recognized as inseparable. For example, in England and Western Europe there was no separation of "elite" and common culture until the sixteenth century, when the powerful realized that by using their power they could pull themselves "above" the so-called masses. In early America, there was less distinction between the levels of society though the Reverend Cotton Mather, though preaching to the masses, detested some of their attitudes and practices. Even Benjamin Franklin, who published for and understood the common people, thought their music very crude and detestable.

But increasingly our culture is coming to realize that the proper study of a democratic society is its democratic cultures and practices, all. Some may be more desirable and respectable, but as Lincoln might have said, some cultures are desirable to some of the people some of the time and as such they are valuable as evidence of that segment of society. This evidence is clearly visible now in the interest we are seeing among archeologists who are digging around in tombs of the dead, not looking for gold but for everyday artifacts.

After you received your Ph.D. from UCLA in 1956, you went on to teach at the University of Maryland and then at Purdue. While at Purdue you hosted the Mid-American Conference in Literature, History, and Folklore in 1965

15

and another conference in 1967. That conference seems a pivotal point in the popular culture movement. Tell me about that time in your life.

I was fortunate to get my first job at the University of Maryland, where Carl Bode was the most influential member of the English Department. He had been in on the founding of the American Studies Association and had urged it to be more inclusive than the mixture of literature, history and philosophy, which it centered on. He was very supportive of my interest in popular culture because that was exactly what he was interested in. He continued to be one of my strongest supporters throughout his life.

In 1960, I went to Purdue, where I found a chair of the department who would support any kind of creative energy, Barriss Mills, and a faculty of young and ambitious people who would help me. Early on at Purdue, I met Russel B. Nye from Michigan State who was at that time interested in all aspects of popular culture and especially young people's literature. Early on, he and I planned to hold a conference on popular culture at Purdue. The administration and faculty were supportive or at least not obstructive.

What made you push for the formation of the Popular Culture Association at the 1967 American Studies Association in Kansas City?

I had been around academia long enough to realize that conferences and associations are vital constituents of success in that world. The two conferences at Purdue were successful. The papers were published or were at least noticed. Ever since going to Purdue, I had planned on establishing a journal of popular culture, though in fact I didn't really know what I was thinking about. Russel Nye thought it a great idea, and I just let the idea simmer. I had been a little pushy in the American Studies Association asking for development in new fields, and when the national meeting was held in Kansas City in 1967 I proposed to the officers that I would host the second meeting in Toledo if they would let me try to establish a Popular Culture Association, again not quite realizing what I was talking about.

What kind of resistance did you encounter when you were first forming the PCA?

The meeting to establish the PCA was exciting. Two hundred of the finest minds at the conference attended the meeting and were enthusiastic about the whole idea. We appointed a couple of officers, or rather I announced myself as secretary-treasurer and Russel Nye as President, and we went on from there. I proudly announced to my colleagues, especially the senior faculty at Purdue, that we had established the PCA and that we would act as a strong assisting arm to the American Studies Association.

Several of them, however, were less enthusiastic than I had expected and explained that in the world of academia nobody helps anybody else but only competes. Though I was convinced of the desire to broaden and assist the American Studies Association, my colleagues have through the years proved right. In academia, ideas seem to be located on territory that has been staked out with "No Trespassing" signs everywhere, and when there is some borrowing, infringing, "rustling," whatever one wants to call it, there is resentment. Despite the fact that academic scholars ride on the backs of footnotes, they seem not to want to expand the general fields of knowledge. At least that seemed to be the case until the study of popular culture forced the American Studies scholars

– and other humanities scholars – to reexamine their fields and attitudes.

Why did you move to Bowling Green State University in 1967? Was the administration supportive of your ideas toward the future development of popular culture studies such as the formation of the *Journal of Popular Culture*?

At Purdue, I had helped a colleague, Donald Winkelman, edit *Abstracts of Folklore*. He went to BGSU because he could get more support there and invited me to come over. I went over to talk to the English Department and Administration and told them I wanted to establish a *Journal of Popular Culture*. All seemed to agree that it was a great idea. I guess I should qualify "all" with "most." They wanted a folklorist and I could masquerade as one.

You were a member of the English department faculty when you first arrived at BGSU. What kinds of problems did you encounter with other faculty members?

A new battle was shaping up at Bowling Green. Once I got there, I started pushing my interest in popular culture and started introducing popular culture into my folklore classes. I was reprimanded several times, but since I had tenure I ignored the reprimands. The faculty grew increasingly restive, but the administration became more and more supportive. The faculty campus-wide also grew more and more polarized. Individuals in several departments were supportive, but mainly the important individuals in all departments were quiet or hostile. Finally, conditions in the English Department became so uncomfortable for all that they told the provost I could not stay in English any longer. He, however, told them that they had to keep me since "nobody else on campus would take me." So I had little recourse but to found my own

18

department – with one colleague. That, however, was not easy. Several chairs of other departments, fearing competition or just out of prejudice, said that the college did not need any more departments, and they would oppose this establishment. The dispute went on for a year until the Dean of Business in disgust finally said that he had had enough of such nonsense: they should found the department and then go on to important business. I always thought he was a wise man.

You were able to establish a master's program in your department, but never a Ph.D. program. Why?

While in English, I had been directing Masters and Ph.D. degrees, and since they needed me they let me continue that course. Because we had only two in Popular Culture, the administration felt that we could hardly give advanced degrees though I continued to direct both in English. Finally, I persuaded the administration to let us give Master's degrees in Popular Culture and was on the verge of getting the Ph.D. when the budget in Columbus was cut and Popular Culture could not hire appropriate faculty for the courses. Now, for at least fifteen years, the establishment of the Ph.D. in Popular Culture has been on hold. It may not come to fruition.

In 1978, you formed the American Culture Association along with the *Journal of American Culture*. Why did you feel that was necessary?

Russel Nye and I spent countless hours talking about how we could make the PCA grow and more nearly accomplish our goals. Each time we agreed that we needed more "respectability," and I was determined to get it. One cold February Sunday morning while I was at home, I hit on the solution: establishment of the American Culture Association and the *Journal of American Culture*. I called Nye to ask him about it, and his answer, as usual, was "Why not?" I then called Carl Bode, who said I should not do it, it was the dumbest idea I had ever had. So, with a vote of two to one, I announced the establishment of both and started to work on them. (It is interesting that some five years after the establishment of the ACA Carl told me one time that he had been wrong in not recognizing its potential.) It was an instant success. Those professors who for one reason or another had not wanted to be caught dirtied by studying popular culture could study American culture and hold their heads up, and publish in JAC, though they had long since been publishing in JPC. Anyway, from the beginning the American Culture Association has been a success though more modified than I had expected. Apparently, the thousands of scholars interested in popular culture want to take it straight, not strained through the sifter of American. JPC still has more than three times as many subscribers as JAC. That is testimony to the strength of the popular culture movement.

In 1988, you published your history of the popular culture movement, *Against Academia*. Why did you feel it was important to publish such a history?

I wrote an "in your face" history because many of the members of the PCA asked me to and because I really wanted the story to be told. I don't know how many people it annoyed, but I do know that it satisfied a lot of members. They were proud of having been a part of such a major movement in academia.

How has your wife, Pat Browne, contributed to the popular culture movement?

I am pleased to say that I have always had a strong helper in all my projects in my wife, Pat. At times, she has opposed an idea, hoped I would not attempt it. But once I have started the motor, she has worked wholeheartedly to make it succeed. She helped me establish and run the Popular Press in 1970, the journals in 1979 and 75, and she has edited her own journal, *Clues*, quite successfully. In 2002, the Midwest Popular Culture Association recognized her many contributions to the study of popular culture, especially in keeping *Popular Music and Society* alive when it had no editor, and her myriad other contributions. She literally has worked day and night, seven days a week to help me and academia mature in popular culture studies.

At the end of your biography written by Gary Hoppenstand and published in *Pioneers in Popular Culture Studies*, Hoppenstand writes, "The more things change, the more they stay the same, unless one makes a Herculean effort to interrupt the circular flow." Have things "stayed the same" for the most part or have significant changes been made in terms of academic acceptance of popular culture studies?

Pat and I have now retired and turned over further development of popular culture studies to other people. We hope our accomplishments have been substantial. During our watch, the humanities have developed from an elitist discipline to a more inclusive one. Now, all aspects of everyday life are being studied in so-called "higher education." That is an opening of the door through which education should and will pass.

What more remains to be done?

The success of the movement now has apparently obviated the need for a Ph.D. degree in the study of popular culture. In academia, the blue ribbon goes with the Ph.D., the

21

department, and holder. But in many colleges and universities to get the authority to grant the Ph.D. one must demonstrate that other schools grant it, and therefore it is needed. Such effort now might be difficult. The study of popular culture is so widespread throughout academia that one can get a Ph.D. in popular culture studies in various other disciplines. So the argument might be made that such a degree in a Popular Culture Department is unnecessary. I believe otherwise. As I read hundreds of papers and books, I see that the study of popular culture is weak in two ways: most people look erroneously upon popular culture as media studies, and many elitists who study popular culture do so wearing gloves, so they won't get their hands dirty. So the study of popular culture should be pursued by properly trained popular culture scholars. Otherwise, the discipline is going to go off on misguided tracks and be forced to be corrected down the road. One of the costly characteristics of Americans is to build now and correct later. Now that the building is in the first stages we should be sure we are laying the correct and lasting foundation.

I wish Pat and I had twenty more years in the vineyard.

FLOYD CHEUNG

Floyd Cheung is an Associate Professor of English and American Studies at Smith College. He is also the founding chair of the Five College Asian/Pacific/American Studies Program. His research and teaching interests include Asian American literature and culture. He has published such articles as "Negative Attraction: The Politics of Interracial Romance in *The Replacement Killers*" in *Americana: The Journal of American Popular Culture* and "Imagining Danger, Imagining Nation: Postcolonial Discourse in *Rising Sun* and *Stargate*" in *Jouvert*. In addition, he has co-edited with Keith Lawrence *Recovered Legacies: Authority and Identity in Early Asian American Literature* (Temple University Press, 2005).

I asked him about the Asian American perspective in American Studies.

What first turned your attention toward American Studies?

Before I turned my attention to American Studies, I was a hardcore student of literature, and in many ways, I still am. In my Las Vegas high school and at Whittier College, I learned to love literature – everything from *The Aeneid* to Jack London. While continuing the study of literature in graduate school, I learned about American Studies from Rebecca Mark, Teresa Toulouse, Amy Kaplan, Donald Weber, and Christopher Benfey, all of whom are also tremendous literary scholars. I have come to think that while nearly all of us believe in approaching the study of American culture from an interdisciplinary perspective, most of us have a particular

23

disciplinary strength. In my case, I try to bring my knowledge of literary traditions, theories, and methods to the field of American Studies.

By the same token, I could not have made as much headway in the recovery of early Asian American literature and culture as I have, if it were not for methods and assumptions that characterize American Studies. For instance, the field's assumption that both high art and popular culture ought to be studied – not to mention that such categories themselves are culturally constructed – helps legitimize the attention that I and others have paid to texts that some in the academy believe to be beneath notice. Take, for instance, the 1887 autobiography of a young, barely-known Asian American named Yan Phou Lee. If we consider Lee's autobiography only as a literary text, it seems not to possess sufficient verbal sophistication or other qualities that most literary scholars value. But when we examine the text from a broader perspective characteristic of American Studies, we see how Lee manipulates the conventions of the slave narrative, the success story, the western adventure tale, and the travel guide in order to intervene in one of the questions of his day: the debate over Chinese exclusion. Since popular conceptions of Chinese at the time as rat-eaters and opium-peddlers helped to justify their oppression, Lee appropriated popular forms familiar to his contemporary readers in an attempt to recuperate the image of the Chinese and improve their treatment in America. Hence, combining disciplinary expertise with American Studies perspectives is sometimes necessary for understanding the significance of works we might otherwise overlook.

Speaking of "texts" that are considered "beneath notice." Did you find that some resisted your interest in popular

culture scholarship, in writing essays on such subjects as *The Replacement Killers*, *Rising Sun*, **and** *Stargate*?

I am unaware of any outright resistance. My colleagues sometimes gently tease me about working on Hollywood action films, but they seem to understand my drive to intervene when I feel it necessary. Of course, I make sure to write about popular texts like *The Replacement Killers* with all of the seriousness and academic rigor that I would apply to more canonical texts. In fact, my interest in taking popular culture seriously parallels my interest in early Asian American literature. In some academic contexts, both categories have been and are undervalued in spite of how much they can illuminate questions about which many of us care.

Tell us more about this "caring." In other words, why do you think it is important for a scholar of Asian American studies to examine American popular culture?

Scholars of Asian American studies know the history of how Asian Americans have been represented and treated in America over the past 150 years, and because we have been trained in a variety of cultural theories, we can identify and study the connections between representation and treatment. For instance, comics, newspaper articles, and films of the 1940s that represented the Japanese and Japanese Americans as untrustworthy, threatening, and alien helped to justify the internment of 120,000 Japanese Americans during World War II and made it easier for the U.S. public to accept the use of atomic bombs on Hiroshima and Nagasaki. Scholars of Asian American studies know, too, the history of how Asian Americans themselves have responded to ill treatment through representing themselves, as well as by seeking legal recourse and taking other kinds of actions. Consequently, it is

25

important for us to examine American popular culture, because we bring to this task bodies of knowledge and theories that aid us in making critical analyses. What might seem like a harmless or isolated representation to an uninformed observer might in fact be a troubling representation that fits into a historical pattern, according to an observer trained in Asian American studies or related field.

What is your view of the image of Asian Americans in American popular culture?

Currently, there are few representations of Asian Americans in mainstream popular culture, and among those only a handful of stereotypical images dominate. I emphasize quantity here, not because quality doesn't matter, but rather because more representations might provide greater opportunities for diversity. For comparison's sake, consider the number of representations of "white" males in U.S. popular culture. (I put *white* in quotation marks, because I understand that term, too – like the term *Asian* or *popular* – to be a constructed and contingent category.) There are enough images of "white" males so that no handful of representations becomes typical. Furthermore, audiences take it for granted that most "white" male characters are complex and have a capacity for change – that they are not representatives of their "race" but rather individuals in their own right. Hence, the character Jack Bauer (played by Kiefer Sutherland) in the television series *24* certainly fits the role of the action hero, but he is also a father distanced from his only daughter, a widower, a patriot, a friend, a rule-breaker, a lover of several women (usually one at a time), an exceptional fighter, and all-around likeable guy. We also accept that he can make mistakes, surprise us, learn, and change. Of course, Jack is not a real person, but he is an individualized character who, to the point, is not defined by his racialized identity, but by his personality and actions. The same cannot be said of most mainstream representations of Asian Americans or, for that matter, most characters of color portrayed in American popular culture.

The theorist Homi Bhabha once argued that the problem with stereotypes is not primarily with whether they are true, false, good, or bad, but rather with their tendency to limit possibilities. This is the case with images of Asian Americans in mainstream American popular culture. We could debate about whether the model minority or yellow peril stereotype dominates in any given text or historical moment. We could discuss whether more Asian Americans are unassimilable foreigners or "new Jews." We could critique vacillating representations of Asian Americans as oversexualized or undersexualized, threatening or docile, whiz kids or Chinatown gangsters. And, to some degree, we should carry on such critiques, since raising awareness of such images, exposing the politics behind them, and understanding how they work rhetorically are important goals. We also ought to point out, however, that more diverse representations are needed so that no handful of types limits the range of possibilities for Asian Americans. Currently, audience expectations with regard to images of Asian Americans are, for the most part, narrow, and consequently the rare Asian American character bears too much of a burden for representing an entire race or ethnicity.

While there are economic and other reasons why there remains such a paucity of Asian American images, I urge more of us to support a greater number and broader range of Asian American representations through – to address the filmgoers among us – seeing movies such as *Saving Face*, *Mississippi Masala*, *Better Luck Tomorrow*, *The Grace Lee*

27

Project, and *Harold and Kumar Go to White Castle.*

In your essay, "Negative Attraction: The Politics of Interracial Romance in *The Replacement Killers*" (2002), you argue that the film "provides an exceptional opportunity for explicating the difference that a racialized identity – specifically, Asian – makes in the production of a late-1990s action film." Tell us more about that.

In that essay, I explained my disappointment with the lack of romance between the two lead characters: John Lee (played by Chow Yun-Fat) and Meg Coburn (played by Mira Sorvino). While the "white" male hero in an action film (recall Indiana Jones, Rambo, or James Bond, for instance) almost always forms a romantic partnership with the female lead – no matter how busy he is fighting bad guys, and no matter her racial identification – Asian and Asian American male characters rarely succeed in this regard. In "Negative Attraction," I argued that this results not from the feminization of Chow's character but rather from the politics of this kind of interracial coupling – namely, an Asian man with a "white" woman. This phenomenon in film history has been aptly described by Gina Marchetti in her book *Romance and the "Yellow Peril": Race, Sex, and Discursive Strategies in Hollywood Fiction.* My contribution to this discussion was to point out how conservative and odd it was for such a history to be repeated in the late 1990s and in a film set in multicultural Los Angeles. Furthermore, I hoped to demonstrate that methods used typically in literary analysis could illuminate the workings of an action film.

Mainstream Hollywood films rarely depict leading men as anything other than normatively masculine and, as part of that definition, heterosexual. If that heterosexuality is not confirmed somehow, then audiences might conclude that the

28

character is not a normative male. Hence, in this film, deployment of the taboo against interracial romance serves also to "feminize" Chow's character. *The Replacement Killers* consequently reinforces a historical pattern: "white" female characters tend not to be attracted to Asian or Asian American male characters, presumably on account of their race but ultimately because there is the suggestion that the male might be nonnormatively male or homosexual (I should add, à la Seinfeld, "not that there's anything wrong with that," except when it serves to exclude Asian and Asian American male characters from the realm of normativity altogether).

Has anything changed since 2002 or do your arguments still hold true?

First, I should say that there are films that came before *The Replacement Killers* that provide exceptions to the generalizations I describe and critique in my essay. For instance, one could cite movies starring Keanu Reeves, who is part-Chinese, part-Hawaiian, and part-English, although he does not self-identify as Asian American. Aside from his films and a few others identified by Marchetti in her book, at least two examples of popular films that feature an interracial romance between an Asian or Asian American male and a "white" female are based on true stories. *Dragon: The Bruce Lee Story* (1993) tells the tale of its title character (played by Jason Scott Lee), including his romance with and marriage to Linda (played by Lauren Holly). Linda, in fact, had penned the biography on which the film was based. Also worth mentioning is *The Ballad of Little Jo* (1993), which my colleague who specializes in Westerns, Alex Keller, recommended to me. Little Jo, as he is known to his surrounding community, is actually Josephine Monaghan (played by Suzy Amis), an exile from her family in the East who finds that the best way to survive as a woman alone in

29

the West is to pass as a man. Eventually, Jo engages in a clandestine affair with a Chinese American man, Tinman Wong (played by David Chung). While their scenes together steam with a sexuality rarely allowed such a pairing, it is poignant to know that their affair could not be public in 1860s Idaho and that those who did find them to make a suitable pair, like their neighbor Frank Badger (played by Bo Hopkins), imagine them as homosexual men. In any case, it is telling that in a world where filmic pairings of Asian or Asian American men with "white" women are few and far between, two of the most high-profile films to feature such pairings are based on true stories, as if to suggest that in such fictions, some measure of "truth" is first required for believability.

Several more recent, purely fictional films also feature an Asian or Asian American man with a "white" woman. For instance, such pairings occur, albeit briefly and even incidentally, in *Better Luck Tomorrow* (2002) and *Harold and Kumar Go to White Castle* (2004). Sometimes, however, these pairings are portrayed in ways that qualify their significance. Consider, for example, *The Tuxedo* (2002), starring Jackie Chan and Jennifer Love Hewitt. In this action-comedy, a taxi driver, Jimmy Tong (played by Chan), dons a technologically marvelous tuxedo that enables him to perform spectacular feats of physical prowess – everything from dancing the mambo to fighting off a horde of enemies. With this tuxedo, Jimmy works as a super-spy à la James Bond with another spy, Del Blaine (played by Hewitt). Together, they must stop a villain who plans to contaminate the world's water supply. Of course, conventions dictate that Jimmy and Del ought to banter, learn to respect each other, and eventually begin a romance. While some viewers have commented that they expect no such romance, given Chan and Hewitt's twenty-five year age difference, we might recall that Sean Connery is twenty-eight years older than Michelle Pfeiffer and thirty-nine years older than Catherine Zeta-Jones, the women who play his characters' lovers in the films *Russia House* and *Entrapment*. In *The Tuxedo*, however, there is nothing more than a friendship suggested in the end, as Jimmy and Del trot off to get a cup of coffee together. Of course, while friendships and other kinds of relationships can be positive and should be valued, it is problematic that Asian American male characters are excluded so consistently from romantic unions. As in the case of *The Replacement Killers*, this outcome is surprising given the publicity surrounding the film. In several interviews, Hewitt fashions herself as a "Chan girl," echoing the well-known term "Bond girl." In the film, Chan's character does introduce himself as "Tong...James Tong," but unlike James Bond, James Tong beds no one. Hence, in this regard, my argument still holds true.

Jimmy's encounter with another "white" woman, Cheryl (played by Mia Cottet), however, flirts with disrupting the taboo against the pairing of an Asian or Asian American male with a "white" female. The potentially taboo-busting sequence of events begins when Jimmy accidentally knocks out James Brown, the Godfather of Soul, just before Brown is supposed to appear on stage at a club where the villain and his fiancée, Cheryl, are in attendance. Since the show must go on, Jimmy replaces Brown and becomes the Last Emperor of Soul. Jimmy is so good (Brown's voice is dubbed in) that Cheryl falls for him and invites him up to her room. Presumably, like a James Bond that must seduce a woman in order to get valuable information from her, Jimmy pretends to countenance Cheryl's affections. But, of course, *The Tuxedo* is not a Bond film; it is an action-comedy with an Asian male lead, and the joke is on Jimmy. He's attractive not because he's himself, but because he performs a technologically-assisted impersonation of James Brown. The audience is supposed to laugh because the "white" female's attraction to

31

singing and dancing marked as "black" is unexpectedly channeled through an Asian body. Jimmy and Cheryl's scene in her hotel room drives home the joke. Her over-the-top lustiness, as she strips and kisses him, overwhelms Jimmy's tenuous attempts at information gathering. (Even the lusty kiss is rendered chaste and funny, however, by its placement on his nose, which leaves a red lipstick mark that enables Del to ask later, "What happened to your nose?") The slapstick rape stops only when Jimmy suggests that she take a bath before they continue; Cheryl assents, saying that indeed she has been a "dirty, dirty girl." The action then moves to another kind of slapstick, as Jimmy – in various states of undress – fights off several attackers. Curiously, the most progressive moment in the film takes place after this fight, when Jimmy and Del hurriedly leave the hotel room. An older couple looks at them and remarks, "Honeymooners. Some things never change." Their comment overlooks the interracial nature of Jimmy and Del's pairing and focuses instead on their heterosexuality and relative youth. As Jimmy and Del run away, Cheryl comes out into the hallway wrapped in a towel. She yells after "The Emperor," but to no avail. Furthermore, she finds that she has locked herself out of her room. Thus ends the sequence, shutting the door on both Cheryl's desire and the film's flirtation with breaking a taboo. Cheryl and Jimmy's potential one-night stand was never more than a misplaced attraction at best and a joke on Jimmy's desirability at worst.

What do you think about the Asian image in other areas of American popular culture – areas other than film?

Simply put, there are too few representations of Asians and Asian Americans in American popular culture, and of those few too many perpetuate stereotypes rather than provide more varied and balanced images. For an excellent list of

32

stereotypes, see Jessica Hagedorn's introduction to *Charlie Chan Is Dead*.

Because of the expense of making feature films and producing television series, backers of these particular media have found it difficult to experiment with more and different depictions of Asians and Asian Americans. The Screen Actors Guild confirms this, reporting in a 6 October 2004 press release that, as the result of economic concerns, the number of Asian or Asian American male leads in primetime shows decreased thirty-five percent from 2002 to 2003. In light of market forces, among other factors, the number and breadth of Asian and Asian American images has improved, if at all, mainly in other kinds of media. The collection *East Main Street: Asian American Popular Culture* – edited by Shilpa Davé, LeiLani Nishime, and Tasha G. Oren – provides an excellent overview and discussion of some of this media ranging from henna tattoos to internet comics. A few of my favorite alternative and interesting, if not altogether unproblematic, representations of Asian Americans in this range of media include the following: the interracial couples in the children's board-book *Everywhere Babies* by Susan Meyers; the internet comic character Secret Asian Man by Tak Toyoshima; musicians including Fred Ho, Vienna Teng, and Yellow Rage; and the comedian Margaret Cho. Of course, Asian American literature presents us with many diverse and thought-provoking images. See *An Interethnic Companion to Asian American Literature* by King-Kok Cheung for an excellent introduction and bibliography.

What are the roots of the problem of how Asians and Asian Americans have been represented in American popular culture?

33

This is a big question, which would require volumes to answer properly, but here I offer a few of the key roots:

Dominant Europeans and Americans, especially before the twentieth century, considered people from the Middle and Far East – or "Orientals," as they sometimes called them – to be their ideological others. These others seemed to have different, at times desirable and at other times threatening, beliefs, customs, behaviors, languages, and attributes. Sometimes, when they have been desirable, they have been labeled as "exotic," and when they have been feared, they have been called "the yellow peril." Some of these older perceptions, desires, and fears persist and can be detected in contemporary stereotypes. (Of course, almost all cultures have their own ways of defining themselves as insiders versus outsiders beyond their borders. The difference in the U.S. case is that our country defines itself as generally welcoming to others. In fact, our Statue of Liberty bids "world-wide welcome," according to Emma Lazarus's famous poem, which is etched on the pedestal on which our torchbearer stands.)

While one of the ideals of our nation is that any immigrant can become an American, for a long time, Asian immigrants have been considered "unassimilable aliens," resistant to change in general and the Americanization process in particular. As a result of this notion, Chinese were denied the opportunity to become naturalized U.S. citizens until 1943; similar laws prevented Japanese from naturalizing until 1952 and other Asian immigrants until 1965. While laws have changed, the assumption persists that those with Asian origins or features are essentially foreigners and never truly Americans. This is why some people ask Asian Americans, "Where are you from?" and answers like New York, Dallas, or Sacramento do not satisfy them. Instead, they seek to confirm their perception of foreignness, fishing with further

34

questions like "No, where are you *originally* from?" or "Where are your parents from?" This preconception also explains why some people insist on complimenting Asian Americans' command of spoken English, even though many of us have grown up speaking the language. This long-standing perception of essential foreignness undergirds many of the ways that Asians and Asian Americans are represented in American popular culture today.

The model minority stereotype has at least two sets of roots. The most recent set of roots harkens back to the 1960s. During the Black Power and Civil Rights Movements, when African Americans and their allies stridently protested and sued for their rights, journalists and pundits searched for a counterargument to the claim that "white" America had oppressed people of color and kept them from advancing in American society. Some constructed the idea of the model minority as one such counterargument. They pointed to Chinese Americans and Japanese Americans in particular to claim that even though these groups had faced various forms of discrimination from exclusion to internment, on the whole members of these groups were doing well in contemporary American society. To explain this, they claimed that Asian cultures value work, education, and the family; furthermore, they argued that members of these cultures succeeded not because they complained but rather because they toiled in silence (see William Peterson's "Success Story of One Minority Group in U.S." in the 26 December 1966 issue of *U.S. News and World Report*, for example). This construction pitched Asian Americans as the "model" for African Americans and others to imitate. In addition, this stereotype served to shift critical attention away from systemic discrimination and inequality. Of course, many scholars, such as Robert S. Chang, subsequently have debunked the

35

logic and evidence used for this construction, but the stereotype lingers nonetheless.

An older set of roots harkens back to the mid-nineteenth century, when immigrant Chinese laborers were employed to build portions of the railroad in the American West. While some employers thought that the Chinese would be too small and weak to perform such arduous labor as laying track, Charles Crocker, a railroad baron, advocated for their use as cheap workers. As it turned out, the Chinese performed admirably. To increase speed, employers sometimes arranged track-building races between Chinese crews and crews composed of other ethnic groups. Also, to promote better behavior and lower expectations among other groups, employers touted the Chinese crews' ability to work for little money and in relative silence. Herein, we see an early version of the model minority stereotype, although it wasn't called this at the time. In the 1800s, some teased these Chinese workers as "Crocker's pets." Of course, historians have debunked this image, too, recovering evidence that Chinese crews did go on strike for better wages and were not the docile pets that some made them out to be.

Interestingly, this early example anticipates a contemporary trend in how the model minority stereotype works hand-in-hand with the yellow peril stereotype. In general, those who stand to gain from Asian Americans, either as an example or as workers, promote them as the model minority, while those who might have something to lose fashion them as the yellow peril. This happened in the nineteenth century, as Crocker touted them as a model and competing workers decried them as a peril. And it happened again in the 1980s, during a perceived crisis with Japanese industry, as some investors praised Japanese business strategies as a model and some U.S. auto workers who lost their jobs saw Asians as a peril. That a few of the latter did not distinguish between Asians and Asian Americans is evidenced tragically in the case of Vincent Chin, a local engineering-firm draftsman who was bludgeoned to death by two "white" auto workers who blamed him for putting them out of work.

The small population of Asian Americans compared with those of other ethnic groups in America has made them convenient scapegoats at various points in history. Also, many Asian Americans' legal and social exclusion from citizenship has muted their political voices. Consequently, without sufficient numbers or votes, they have been historically vulnerable to misrepresentation and unfair treatment. On this score, one need only think of Japanese Americans during the 1940s, one-third of whom were not citizens thanks to U.S. immigration laws. They were incarcerated during World War II, while their German and Italian American counterparts were treated much more like individuals and less like a monolithic group.

Finally, Asian Americans don't actually compose a coherent category or voting bloc in America, in spite the racialist notion that "all Orientals look alike" and the fact that the U.S. government has constructed the category of "Asian or Pacific Islander." More than fifteen different ethnicities fit under the broad rubric of "Asian American," and while these disparate people have formed a coalition in some cases, their diversity – with regard to both identities and interests – often has mitigated their ability to counter problematic representations and treatment in a unified way. Hence, I would consider Asian Americans' diversity not as a root of the problem but as a significant reason why the problem has been difficult to solve.

37

For more on the roots of the problem of how the Middle East has been represented, see Edward Said's *Orientalism*. For a history of how representations of Asians and Asian Americans have evolved, see Robert G. Lee's *Orientals: Asian Americans in Popular Culture*. And for a study of Asian American voting patterns, see Pei-Te Lien's *The Political Participation of Asian Americans: Voting Behavior in Southern California*.

SHELLEY FISHER FISHKIN

Professor Shelley Fisher Fishkin is the Joseph S. Atha Professor of Humanities, Professor of English, and the Director of the American Studies Program at Stanford University. She holds a Ph.D. from Yale University in American Studies and has won many awards including an American Council of Learned Societies Fellowship, a Fulbright, a Frank Luther Mott/Kappa Tau Alpha Award, and the Harry H. Ransom Teaching Excellence Award; she is also a Life Member of Clare Hall at Cambridge University. She has authored, edited, or co-edited over forty books as well as publishing over 100 articles. Some of her most outstanding books are *From Fact to Fiction: Journalism and Imaginative Writing in America* (Johns Hopkins University Press, 1985), *Was Huck Black?: Mark Twain and African-American Voices* (Oxford University Press, 1993), *Lighting Out for the Territory: Reflections on Mark Twain and American Culture* (Oxford University Press, 1997), *Feminist Engagements: Forays into American Literature and Culture* (Palgrave Macmillan, 2009), and the twenty-nine volume *Oxford Mark Twain* (Oxford University Press, 1996). She co-produced an adaptation of Mark Twain's play *Is He Dead?*, which premiered at the Lyceum Theatre on Broadway in 2007. Her current work includes recovery of the experiences and voices of Chinese workers who built the transcontinental railroad.

I asked her about her Mark Twain scholarship.

When did you first know you would study and write about Twain? What attracted you to the man and his work?

I had a passing acquaintance with some of Twain's

entertaining short fiction as a child, but had never thought of him as a writer with serious things to say. During my junior year in high school, my teacher handed out copies of *Huckleberry Finn* and announced that we would be writing papers on "how Twain used irony to attack racism." After I got over my surprise, I found the challenge of writing that paper exhilarating. Reading between the lines, probing what the author, as opposed to the narrator, was trying to do, was enormously stimulating. The book also gave me more insight into the dynamics of racism, American style, than anything on the evening news or the daily paper.

Writing that paper made me discover how much I liked writing about literature and made me decide to be an English major in college. But the Yale English department was obsessed with British – not American – literature in those days, and that obsession shaped the structure of the major. As an Intensive English Major at Yale, I had exactly one course in American literature. Twain wasn't in it. In short, I forgot about Twain during college, despite the fact that he had prompted me to go into literary studies in the first place. But I returned to him when I decided to get my Ph.D. in American Studies rather than English. He was one of five writers in my dissertation project and the book that came out of it: *From Fact to Fiction: Journalism and Imaginative Writing in America*.

My first wild adventure with Twain happened shortly before that book was published. I was infuriated by the efforts of a black educator named John Wallace to close down a production of *Huck Finn* at the Goodman Theatre in Chicago, and to take the book out of the nation's schools, on the grounds that the novel and its author were racist. (He wanted to replace Twain's book with his own edition of it – which, like the recent New South Books edition, replaced every use of the word "nigger" with "slave.") I wrote an op-ed that the *New York Times* published on the 100th anniversary of the publication of *Huck Finn* in the U.S. I observed that Mark Twain had had to turn to satire in the first place because his direct exposés of racism (towards the Chinese in San Francisco) were censored; but now he faced the prospect of censorship once again because some readers couldn't understand his irony. The day that op-ed appeared in the *Times*, I was awakened by a phone call. A woman said, "I don't know you, but I just read your piece in the *New York Times*, and I've got to see you right away. I have a letter Mark Twain wrote that nobody knows about yet, and after reading your column, I know you'll know what to do with it. Here's what it says." She read me the letter over the phone. A chill went through me as I realized that the letter contained the only direct, non-ironic condemnation of racism that we had from Twain during the period in which he published *Huck Finn*. Indeed, it was written the same year that *Huck Finn* was published. The woman who called me was an antiques dealer who had found it in an old desk. I authenticated the letter and I researched its context single-mindedly over the next few weeks, reconstructing a story that ended up intriguing others as much as it fascinated me: Warner T. McGuinn, the young black law student Twain wrote about in the letter, a young man whom he would end up funding through his own private "affirmative action" plan, went on to become a major civil rights lawyer who was a mentor to Thurgood Marshall. The story (which the *New York Times* ran on its front page) got huge national and international attention.

Your book *Was Huck Black? Mark Twain and African-American Voices* made you an academic star. What are your reflections on the publication of the book and reception now?

The seeds for that book were planted when I heard the award-winning novelist David Bradley, author of *The Chaneysville Incident* (my candidate for the great American novel of our time) give a talk at a New England American Studies Association conference that he provocatively called "The First 'Nigger' Novel." He said, "You folks know a lot about Sam Clemens. Sam Clemens was white. But who here among you has ever seen Mark Twain? Mark Twain was black." He then proceeded to make a case for *Huckleberry Finn* as a work which prefigured the fiction of black writers in the twentieth century – including his own. The audience, to put it mildly, was in shock. Some were outraged. Others were simply confused. My own response? He was definitely onto something...the seeds that were planted that night took six or seven years to germinate.

Black writers who admired Twain included Charles Chesnutt, who kept a bust of Twain in his library, and Langston Hughes and Richard Wright, both of whom paid eloquent homage to Twain in print. Through conversations and correspondence over the next few years, I found that Twain had been important to other contemporary black writers besides Bradley, including Toni Morrison, who returned to Twain when she was honing her craft as a writer. It was during an interview with Ralph Ellison in 1991 that my own variation on Bradley's theory began to take shape. After showing me the photo of Twain that hung over his desk, Ellison spoke of Twain's special appreciation of the vernacular and of the irony at the core of a nation founded on ideals of freedom that tolerated slavery and racism in its midst. Mark Twain, Ellison said, "made it possible for many of us to find our own voices." *Why* had Twain played this empowering role for black writers? I wondered aloud. Could some of the things Ellison learned from Twain be things Twain himself had learned from the rhetorical performances of African Americans? Yes,

42

Ellison told me, "I think it comes full circle." From that moment on, I began to systematically track all black speakers mentioned or quoted in Mark Twain's work. One piece was an obscure article Twain had written in the *New York Times* in 1874 about a ten-year-old black child named Jimmy who had impressed him as "the most artless, sociable, exhaustless talker" he had ever come across, someone to whom he had listened, "as one who receives a revelation." I found compelling evidence that black speakers had played a central role in the genesis not only of Twain's black characters, but of his most famous white one: Huckleberry Finn. I was bursting with excitement about this research and chose to speak about it when I was invited to give a talk at Princeton in early 1992. Toni Morrison, who was then in the process of writing *Playing in the Dark*, came to my talk and asked whether she could join those of us going to dinner afterwards.

At dinner, she gave me my marching orders: drop whatever else you're doing and write a book about *this*. This is more important than anything else you could do, she told me. I decided to take her advice. But doing so was a little scary. If black speakers and oral traditions had played such an important role in shaping Twain's art, why hadn't anyone noticed it before, given the literally thousands of books and articles on Twain that had appeared? Soon I noticed a pattern: literary scholars had denied any African-American influence on mainstream American texts much as linguists had denied any African-American influence on Southern speech and American speech in general. All of them, I became increasingly convinced, were wrong. I mined published and unpublished fiction, nonfiction, and speeches by Twain and by black contemporaries; folklore and linguistic studies; history, newspapers, letters, manuscripts, and journals. I didn't come up for air all spring. Decades earlier, Ellison had written that "the black man" was the "co-creator of the

language Mark Twain raised to the level of literary eloquence."
But literary historians ignored him and continued to tell us
that white writers came from white literary ancestors and
black writers from black ones. I knew that story had to change
if we wanted to do justice to the richness of our culture. I'm
delighted that my research and the book that resulted – *Was
Huck Black? Mark Twain and African-American Voices* –
helped make that change happen. I was somewhat astonished
by the ruckus it caused! Why should people have been so
surprised by the idea that black and white writers and
speakers had been shaping each other's work throughout our
nation's history? Segregated lunch counters may have
disappeared in the 1960s, but segregated syllabi were still
alive and well in the 1990s. In the early 1990s, there were
"American Literature" courses, which were populated almost
completely by "white" writers, and there were "African-
American Literature Courses" that focused on writers who
were invariably "black." My book challenged the usefulness n
– and accuracy – of those segregated silos.

I've just returned from a really exciting exploratory workshop
at the Radcliffe Institute organized by Glenda Carpio, Jeffrey
Ferguson, and Werner Sollors to brainstorm about a new
anthology of American literature that will make breaking
down these "silos" a central goal. I'm delighted to be a part of
that project! If I were to have the chance to write *Was Huck
Black? Mark Twain and African-American Voices*, again, I
would do one thing differently: I would explain the title. It
was a mistake to assume that everyone would know that my
title was signifying on the "one-drop rule." Some of my critics
ridiculed my argument by charging me with denying that any
white voices had shaped Huck's voice in the book, which is
preposterous. My title was simply playing with the idea that if
we applied the "one-drop rule" to culture, and if Huck's voice
was shaped at least in part by black voices, then Huck was

44

"black." I should have said so.

So Twain was also a playwright.

Yes. And an eminently forgettable one, for the most part! I needed to check something in one of his plays, and when I went to find it at the Mark Twain Papers, I was amazed that there was an entire file-drawer full of them! Most were pretty awful. But I decided to eat my scholarly spinach and read through the whole damned mess. It was a really rough slog. (Typical, and probably, although not necessarily the worst, was a melodrama about Oliver Cromwell.)

But virtue was rewarded: the penultimate play in the drawer – an amanuensis copy of a manuscript that had never been transcribed – was *Is He Dead? A Comedy in Three Acts*. I burst into laughter several times as I read through it. It was totally unexpected: a wild, cross-dressing farce set in France about outwitting a mean and unremitting creditor that Twain began writing the week he learned that he had finally come out of bankruptcy.

I was not the first scholar to read *Is He Dead?*, but I was the first to see its potential. In my mind's eye, I could see it on stage. I suspected it would be as much fun to watch as it was to read. There were some amazing scenes that reprised some comic gambits Twain had experimented with earlier but not fully realized until now. I was determined to get it published (that was the easy part – the University of California Press was happy to have me do that) – and to get it performed. That turned out to be harder. I sought permission from the Mark Twain Foundation (who owned the dramatization rights to the play) to get it produced. They agreed – and asked me to represent them, and Twain, in that process.

45

Tell us about your experience bringing *Is He Dead?* to the stage.

I went around asking everyone I knew if they knew how to get a play produced. Nobody did. Until I asked an old friend, Dan Werner, who was executive producer of the *PBS Newshour* with Jim Lehrer, and who had collaborated with my husband on a number of projects. Dan said that he knew someone who would know: Bob Boyett, a close friend of Jim Lehrer's and a Broadway producer. Bob was willing to read the manuscript. A few months later, when I was visiting family on the East coast, Bob asked me to lunch. I figured he would recommend that I contact the artistic director of a good regional theatre. He shocked me by saying he wanted to produce it himself!

Bob knew that the play would need a good play-doctor. (Twain knew this, as well, and mused about trying to get a friend in New York to find him one. But he never did.) After all, the three acts needed to be pared down to two if it was to work on the stage today. And the play as Twain wrote it would have required thirty-five actors. After a table reading with actors in Bob's New York office, he came up with the perfect "collaborator" for Twain: playwright David Ives, who is renowned not only for his own comic brilliance as a playwright (*All in the Timing*, and many other plays), but for his ability to adapt classic musicals to contemporary tastes in the "Encore!" series in New York.

It was a little daunting to be the person "standing in for" Mark Twain over the next couple of years, as David Ives worked on the script. He brought extraordinary skill and élan to the venture, miraculously turning the play into one that eleven actors could perform (with some doubling). He "punched up" parts here and there, brought a scene onstage that Twain had

46

offstage, added some jokes of his own, and generally made it a much better play.

I needed to approve every line that was changed from the original. Most of Ives's ideas were inspired, but not all. Out of respect for Twain's original choice, I wouldn't go along with changing the artist at the center of the play from Jean-Francois Millet to someone better-known in the U.S. today, like Renoir or Van Gogh. I also wouldn't let him change the play's title. And at times I felt like a card-carrying member of the anachronism police. But by and large, I was in awe of Ives's gifted efforts to adapt Twain for the twenty-first century stage.

When Bob signed on the brilliant director Michael Blakemore (the only director to win Tonys for Best Play and Best Musical in one season), I was thrilled. Getting to be a Broadway producer was the ultimate "Walter Mitty" dream for a college professor like myself. I loved answering questions from the cast at some of the early rehearsals, getting to know an incredibly talented group of actors, learning behind the scenes about the details that go into securing historically-accurate props, holding talkbacks in the theatre after a number of the performances – even coping with the brutal economic realities of Broadway with my fellow producers on the show. And, of course, sharing the pleasure that the other producers, the cast, and the director felt when all those rave reviews came in.

During the four years since the show closed on Broadway, there have been well over 200 productions of *Is He Dead?* around the country and around the world.

I've seen professional productions of the play in the L.A. and Washington, DC areas (at the International City Theatre in

47

Long Beach and the Olney Theatre Center in Maryland), a high school production in northern California, and a college production at Yale. It's wonderful to see a play that Twain had so much fun writing getting audiences to laugh so much over a century after his death! I hated having to miss the performances mounted in Russia, Romania, and Sri Lanka.

We can't leave Twain behind. Here, in the twenty-first century, audiences are still fascinated by his work. Why is this so? How does he remain so relevant in American culture a century or so later?

Twain wears well. His language remains fresh and lively, his subjects often seem ripped from today's headlines, and he makes readers today laugh as much as he made readers laugh in his own day. But it's more than that: there's a keen moral sensibility underlying so much of what he wrote. Twain wrote that "humor must not professedly teach, and it must not professedly preach, but it must do both if it would live forever." His does both – with a subtlety and grace that is as inimitable as it is enviable. He also zeroed in on some of the fault lines in American culture with a sense of perfect pitch that none have equaled, before or after. He knew us "by the back" (to borrow an expression Jim used in *Huck Finn*); he claimed to be able to paint our flaws as convincingly as he did because he shared them. He still challenges us – to be our best selves, to live up to our ideals, to figure out exactly how his books have the effect on us that they have.

Where do you hope to go next in your Twain studies?

I'm intrigued by Twain as a global author. When I edited *The Mark Twain Anthology* for the Library of America recently, I was stunned to find a vast body of writing on Twain in languages other than English. (I ended up getting pieces by

48

great writers from around the world translated for the book from Chinese, Danish, French, German, Italian, Japanese, Russian, Spanish, and Yiddish.) I've become fascinated by understanding how a book like *Huck Finn* gets translated, and the cultural work that those translations do. I'm also fascinated by Twain as a citizen of the world – as Howells once put it, "Originally of Missouri…now of the universe."

SAM B. GIRGUS

Sam B. Girgus is a Professor of English at Vanderbilt University with special interests in philosophy, ethics, film, and American Studies. He has received several prestigious honors including the Rockefeller Humanities Fellowship and Senior Fulbright Lectureship. His many books include *The American Self: Myth, Ideology, and Popular Culture* (University of New Mexico Press, 1981), *The Films of Woody Allen* (Cambridge University Press, 1993, 2002), *The Hollywood Renaissance: The Cinema of Democracy in the Era of Ford, Capra, and Kazan* (Cambridge University Press, 1998), *America on Film: Modernism, Documentary, and a Changing America* (Cambridge University Press, 2002), and the recently released *Levinas and the Cinema of Redemption: Time, Ethics, and the Feminine* (Columbia University Press, 2010).

I asked him about his career as an Americanist in literature and film studies.

You started out in American Studies, moved to English, then Film Studies. Talk to us about these turns.

I suppose that all of these "turns" exhibit what in American Studies we used to call an eclectic or what Henry Nash Smith dubbed an "opportunistic" approach to studying and analyzing changing issues about culture and history. They indicate a kind of pragmatic attitude toward methodology, the attempt to invent a systematic approach to problems so that ends and means cohere. At its core, I suppose it also goes back to a basic insistence on rigorous research as part of a method of investigation that deals with issues from diverse perspectives.

When I started out as a professor and scholar, I saw my first passion as American culture and the American experience as opposed to a commitment to a specific discipline such as literature or history. So I went into American Studies. In time, I also became deeply interested in Freud and psychoanalysis as part of an attempt to understand American culture. I was very influenced by the work of Christopher Lasch as a way to meld history, psychoanalysis, and literature. Then, when I felt I had written all I could in American literature and when the discipline itself seemed to be changing, I began to pursue my interests by studying film and more recently philosophy and ethics.

Do you see your career in the Navy as influencing your scholarship in any way? Likewise, you've done a lot of work abroad as a scholar and teacher. Presumably, that experience affected you as an American Studies scholar as well?

I think any experience that exposes you to a diversity of people and relationships should prove beneficial for opening and deepening perspectives and understandings. The benefit I received from that very undramatic military experience in the 1960s was the association with people from all kinds of places and backgrounds with so much to offer.

The teaching and scholarly work abroad proved life changing – especially first-hand experience over several years in Eastern Europe and even in the last days of the Soviet Union. These events definitely solidified, probably as it was meant to, my adherence to a classic view of the meaning of the American idea and experience to the world. In Hungary, in Poland, in Bulgaria, in Moscow just steps away from the Kremlin, I met so many people who felt lost and hopeless in their own time and place and looked to America, truly in

51

Lincoln's words, as "the last best hope."

In 1982, you edited *The American Self: Myth, Ideology, and Popular Culture* with essays from such luminaries as Sacvan Bercovitch, Henry Nash Smith, and John Cawelti. What's your biggest "take away" from such a distinguished collection of essays?

I was and remain very proud of that work and especially was happy that it was representative not just of a collection of scholars but of a philosophy and approach to education and teaching American culture studies at both the undergraduate and graduate levels. The collection indicated what we were doing in the classroom and as an institutional program. In addition, it was intended to suggest an academic community of scholars and students and learners. At the same time, it was, I think, a vital and valuable collection of major scholarship and criticism in American Studies. Saki's essay in *The American Self* was a seminal piece that helped initiate the importance for the field of the whole idea of the "ideology of consensus." Equally important, along with such figures as Henry Nash Smith, Saki, Walter Blair, and Alan Trachtenberg, *The American Self* also included the work of new and rising scholars such as a young African-American scholar who now is my colleague at Vanderbilt – Houston Baker. I have teased Houston since he came to Vanderbilt that if I knew how important and influential he would become that I would have placed the essay better. In addition, long before I ever thought that I would be writing about film, the essay included important work by Bob Sklar. I continue to go back to Bob's essay in that collection on *It's a Wonderful Life* in the new book on the "cinema of redemption." Perhaps the most important and lasting lesson, however, is laced with irony in that the great glow that emanated from the power of the light from such, as you say "luminaries," blinded me to how

52

quickly and deeply the whole field was undergoing transformation. At that point, I still believed in the idea of American Studies as a big tent that covered a community of diverse interests.

So the irony for me that emerges from the collection is the basic one of being prepared for change and not being so surprised by it even when it takes place right in front of you, and you don't recognize it as something that also will be changing your life. So with the publication of my first three books on American literature, I was looking at a field that seemed to be changing and moved to apply my basic interests and passions about American culture to a new field and discipline that was fresh and unexplored for me at the time – maybe a "virgin land" of academic opportunity.

Then American Studies as a field moved as far away as possible, as far as I could tell, from my kind of thinking about the American experience. Some people wrote about the new wave as a kind of anti-American Studies. So for me the "big tent" idea of American Studies that was so important for housing and nurturing inclusion, pluralism, and diversity seemed to collapse and change, depending I guess on how you felt about who was in and who was out of the tent. For many, the ideology of consensus and its academic applications were themselves restrictive, confining, and limiting. Such critics wanted to change the boundaries and structures of the discourse, whereas I felt a loss of the very instruments, ideas, and values of pluralism, diversity, and debate that had made the country and the discipline work.

When I began studying, teaching, and writing about American literature and American Studies, I approached those fields with the idea at the time of America as a unique experience in human history. That was what made the study of the culture

53

and history so exciting and worthwhile. It was not just a matter of cultural anthropology or the studious and rigorous analysis of an exciting historical narrative. American literature was a crucial part of that unique experience. In fact it manifested, articulated, and advanced that experience. As Saki argues, the idea of America was what American literature was all about. Significantly, this notion of uniqueness, was what we also used to call American "exceptionalism."

American exceptionalism at that time meant nothing like its uses in recent political discussion as crude and vulgar examples of American chauvinism and super-patriotism and arrogance – although for sure our history unfortunately has undergone many prolonged instances of such perversions of the idea of American mission. However, exceptionalism was taken to mean at the time, according to my understanding, the idea of America as an ideology – an "ism" – "Americanism" unlike any other nation in the world – Britain, the Soviet Union or Russia, Israel. Exceptionalism referred to America as an invented national entity. America was called "the first universal nation." America was an asylum and sanctuary for all peoples from all over the world. We could recite the words of Paine, Jefferson, Crevecoeur, who helped to implant that idea, and of course Lincoln, who used it to perpetuate "the last best hope of earth" in the face of the Civil War, and Roosevelt and Eisenhower and Kennedy who revived and sustained it to inspire the contests against Nazi and Soviet totalitarianism.

To my thinking and study, what made that idea work was what Gunnar Myrdal called an "American Creed" that was basically an ideology of ethical relationships of fairness, equality, opportunity, democracy. It was supposed to mean that everyone had a chance to participate in the system. To the extent that we failed to live up to that creed, the ideology of

54

exceptionalism failed. In other words, an ethical obligation that Saki traced back to the "American Jeremiad" of the Puritans was the glue that kept it together with an ever-expanding vision of inclusion.

Dissent and difference were intrinsic to this system and indispensable to making it work. This is what Saki called "dissensus" as a key part of the ideology of consensus in America. So to me the American idea, as I argue in the new *Levinas and the Cinema of Redemption*, was all about ideological dissensus long before the term came to be used by some left-leaning critics today as part of their own projects for change, reform, and renewal. Dissensus in relation to the American idea, however, is not just an abstract notion or proposal, but entails a practice and politics with a history that can be studied and criticized and perhaps used and emulated as a foundation for greater change in conjunction with more contemporary ways of thinking.

At some point, it seemed to become politically incorrect, unfashionable or just old fashioned to see things this way. In addition, there was this great surge of powerful new theoretical languages and critical approaches to literature that many felt were important to use in the classroom. Not that I hid or disguised my views or avoided expressing them. So I moved over to film, where I thought my approach would be somewhat newer to that field and where these ideas about American culture had not been tested so extensively as far as I knew. I ventured into new, unexplored territory – at least for me. As research, criticism, and scholarship, my books are meant to provide the basis for the claims and arguments that are made in the classroom about film and culture. Perhaps it's really just a case of self-exile so that I can watch, teach, and write about the films I have loved all my life.

When you turned to film, you turned first to Woody Allen. What do American Studies scholars need to understand about this filmmaker?

When I started that book, the argument that was a bit original at the time was to emphasize the genius and originality of Allen as a filmmaker as opposed to simply seeing him as a comic genius making movies. The seriousness of that study of him I think was important at that time as was the effort to see Allen as part of an American literary and cultural tradition that also included humor, ethnicity, and film.

After going through several translations, the book now is in a second edition which is funny to me personally because in the intervening years I have developed a more distant, critical view of Allen. So the new chapters in the second edition reflect some changes in my perception and thinking about him. I argue first of all that in the wake and light of the scandal involving Soon-Yi Previn, the aura surrounding his image as the beloved and admired funny New York Jewish comic genius collapsed and this radically affected his art in his films. He was no longer able to use his on-screen image and persona to fulfill his art. He lost the basic vehicle that ignited and moved the humor, narrative, and character development of his films. For one thing, it was hard to continue portraying himself as the basically decent, ethical but all too human and flawed schlemiel-like victim of others. So trying to get Kenneth Branagh to fill in for him in *Celebrity* or playing himself as a crude, negative figure in *Deconstructing Harry* were to me failures and signs of that crisis in his creativity.

Significantly, his recent films that I consider so good such as *Match Point* and *Vicky Cristina Barcelona* take place outside of New York and without him in the starring role. Also, in the years between the two editions of *The Films of Woody Allen*

56

during which I kept up with his work and career, I guess I became disillusioned about his ability to manipulate so much of the New York and even national media. It made him seem contrived and inauthentic, the very opposite of the qualities that made him so effective in his classic films and comedy.

In 1998, you published *The Hollywood Renaissance: The Cinema of Democracy in the Era of Ford, Capra, and Kazan* **with Cambridge University Press. You believe that these filmmakers "replicate the situation of our classic Renaissance writers in dramatizing the basic values, conflicts, and contradictions of American democracy." Tell us more about those connections.**

I still care deeply about this book and am glad that it is apparently still in print – at least I still make my students buy and read it. In the book, I try to propose that Saki's idea of American consensus, jeremiad, and mission as part of a culture of dissensus carried over from the time of the so-called "American Renaissance" to the work of the great directors of the "Hollywood Renaissance," a term borrowed from others.

This meant to me that the genius of these great directors – Ford, Capra, Kazan, Hawks, Stevens – others not emphasized such as Wyler, Sturges, Wellman – was to see, when it came to the American experience, that the dialogue of dissensus and consensus rather than intellectual and ethical conformity characterizes the so-called "exceptionalism" of America.

Film begins to change and you document that in 2002 with *America on Film*. **Talk to us about the tensions concerning race and gender.**

The chapters in *America on Film* attempt to see important

films such as *Mississippi Masala* (Mira Nair the director with that wonder and genius of acting today, Denzel Washington), *Lone Star*, and *Malcolm X* as part of the broader American experience, while other chapters also emphasize the importance of seeing sexuality and gender as crucial in the construction of subjectivity and cultural identity.

Why did you write *Levinas and the Cinema of Redemption: Time, Ethics, and the Feminine*? Levinas is so important for someone concerned with philosophy and ethics, as you are. He advocated the "wisdom of love" rather than the "love of wisdom" and believed in "ethics as first philosophy."

I became obsessed with the importance of Levinas's ethical philosophy of placing a priority on the face of the other as opposed to the existential self. It was an extreme reversal for me of customary ways of thinking about individualism, personal identity, and freedom that also made sense as an irreducible source of ethics based on inter-subjective relations. It made me realize that in a way the book and idea are an extension or counterpart to *Hollywood Renaissance* by identifying the source of ethics not just in culture and society but in alterity and the relationship to the other. Levinas says in *Totality and Infinity*, "Everyone will readily agree that it is of the highest importance to know whether we are not duped by morality." That seemed to me to be a key question for Capra and Ford and other directors. Moreover, the key concepts for Levinas of time and the feminine as inexorably connected to ethical relationships and subjectivity also seemed to have a strong potential for providing an interesting way to study film.

So Levinas in a way brings me back to American Studies. Interestingly, I see some similarity between Levinas's idea of the mission of Israel, meaning the idea or ideal of the

58

messianic Israel as the heavenly city incarnate, and my sense of America's place and role in the world. Obviously, such notions are anathema to some today and have become the object of ridicule and condemnation to such critics.

Now writing about Levinas and ethics as informing American transcendence and the cinema of redemption suggests to me a foundation of ethics and responsibility for both the *American Renaissance* and the *Hollywood Renaissance*. Reading Levinas put Matthiessen's *American Renaissance* and the *Hollywood Renaissance* in new contexts for me with historic foundations that integrate ethics and transcendence.

You return again and again to that word "ethics."

In retrospect, ethics seem to me to run through everything that I write about including exceptionalism, the Jeremiad, the American Creed, the rhetoric and ideology of American mission. It is rather amazing and exciting to me how what we used to call "the life of the mind" can be so rejuvenating and revivifying as ideas relate and develop over the years. The new book, *Levinas and the Cinema of Redemption*, involved opening a whole new area for me of philosophy, ethics, and phenomenology. In fact, some readers generously have claimed that the book also opens a new direction and interest in film study. However, at some point toward the end of the project, I realized, as I said, that when I was writing *Hollywood Renaissance*, I in fact also was working on the ideas and problems for the *Cinema of Redemption*, although at the time, of course, I didn't quite know it. In other words for me, after discussing the sources in American culture, history, literature, and ideology that went into the making of the so-called "Hollywood Renaissance," I came to appreciate more fully that there also existed another dimension and source that involve the issue of ethics and transcendence. Levinas

59

articulates this dimension in our time in Continental philosophy, but closer to home in America, the Puritans, and the Transcendentalists, of course, were committed to such concepts as regeneration, redemption, and transcendence in their different ways and discourse.

WILLIAM A. GLEASON

William A. Gleason holds a Ph.D. in English from UCLA and serves as full professor as well as chair of the Department of English at Princeton University. He has received numerous awards including a grant from the National Endowment for the Humanities and has published two books: *The Leisure Ethic: Work and Play in American Literature, 1840-1940* (Stanford University Press, 1999) and *Sites Unseen: Architecture, Race, and American Literature* (New York University Press, 2011).

I asked him about his interest in American Studies, his two books, and the concept of space in his work.

What attracted you to late nineteenth-early twentieth century American Studies?

I've always been fascinated by this period – probably dating back to an American literature course I took in high school – but it was in graduate school at UCLA that my scholarly interest in the era really took shape. I think it's the tumult. These are years of incredible social, economic, and political upheaval, from the Civil War and Reconstruction, through the Gilded Age and the Progressive Era, into the Roaring Twenties and the Depression. And of course it's an age of cultural upheaval, too, with an explosion of print culture, on the one hand, and the rise of new media like film and radio, on the other. As someone deeply interested in the ways that cultural forms emerge from and also help shape their historical moments, this has always struck me as an exceptionally rich period to do the kind of contextual and interdisciplinary work that I enjoy most. For helping nurture

61

this interest, I would also have to thank the Americanist faculty who taught such wonderful courses in this period while I was at UCLA, including Martha Banta, Eric Sundquist, Valerie Smith, and Richard Yarborough, plus folks like Michael Colacurcio, Ken Lincoln, Barbara Packer, and Stephen Yenser, from whom I learned so much about making culture and history speak to each other.

You teach a graduate seminar called The Rise of the Popular. Can you tell us a little about the "thesis" of the course?

The course really has two implicit arguments. First, that popular writing in the U.S. comes of age between roughly 1790 and 1900, by which I mean that many of the most familiar popular American literary genres – sentiment, gothic, seduction, adventure, reform – emerge, develop, and in many cases consolidate during this period. (Paul Gutjahr's *Popular American Literature of the Nineteenth Century* anthology is perfect for this course, although because I now use more full-length texts than excerpts I've made it a reference work rather than the main volume.)

The second argument of the course is that this "rise" needs to be understood in relation to key shifts in the social, economic, and legal dimensions of reading and publishing as well as developments in popular culture more broadly. So we also study changes in U.S. publishing practices and the history of the book. As a result, the course has become more and more archival. When I taught the seminar most recently this past spring, I worked with our rare books librarian each week to develop a kind of hands-on "display case" of texts and objects that would supplement our primary readings. The librarian brought these materials into the seminar, usually just after the midpoint break, for the students to handle and discuss. These materials could range from other examples of the literary genre under review, to popular prints or lithographs, to other items like sheet music, handbills, or even toys.

I was pleased to see several students choose archival research projects for their end-of-semester work. That's another goal of the course: not just to introduce students to archival research but also to get them interested in trying it themselves.

In *The Leisure Ethic*, you write about the concept of leisure and leisure space as a kind of new frontier. What were the central issues at stake in that debate?

The play theorists and recreation reformers I write about in *The Leisure Ethic* saw leisure very much as Frederick Jackson Turner saw the western frontier: as a potentially revitalizing space of freedom, self-invention, and democracy. They even used many of the same metaphors for the power of play that Turner used for the frontier. They felt that play, for example, provided a "safety valve" for the release of pent-up energies, which is exactly how Turner (rightly or wrongly) talked about the frontier's role in defusing economic and social competition in a rapidly urbanizing nation.

What the play theorists wanted to do, in effect, was bring the energies of Turner's frontier – supposedly "closed" as of 1893 – back *into* the city, by designing spaces (such as urban playgrounds) that would let children, and especially boys, experience the exuberant freedoms supposedly denied them by the demands of urban life. This kind of play, they argued, would provide the city child with precisely the kinds of skills (physical, intellectual, moral) that rural life, felt to be precipitously on the wane, formerly nurtured.

There were a number of issues at stake in this reformulation.

63

For one, not everyone agreed that "city life" was as stultifying as the play theorists proposed. Critics of the reformers pointed to the exuberance of unsupervised street play, particularly in densely populated immigrant neighborhoods, as an example of urban recreation that already produced the kind of freedom and improvisation the theorists hoped to bring to life in city parks and playgrounds. This critique had a particular charge because the play theorists focused much of their own energies on immigrants – both children and adults – whom they felt could be properly Americanized through directed play, magically transformed from ethnic "outsiders" to assimilated "insiders" by means of quintessentially American team games like baseball.

This debate also pointed to one of the ironies of play theory. Though reformers championed the freedoms of modern play over the constraints of modern work, the playgrounds they imagined required careful supervision, guidance, and instruction. "Proper" play, for the reformers, was more important than simply free play.

This interest in proper play brought the reformers into another debate that erupted with special force with the emergence of modern forms of commercial leisure. In my book, I call this the "play debate" of the 1920s, and it pitted play theorists against commercial distributors of leisure, including motion picture studios, stage companies, and collegiate and professional sports. Play reformers decried such forms of popular leisure as passive rather than active and as focused on spectacle rather than participation. In this debate, many others, including religious leaders, criminologists, and psychologists, joined the reformers in cautioning against the misuse of leisure. In *The Leisure Ethic*, I show how American writers joined this debate as well, through stories that assailed not only passive spectatorship but also the play theorists' reconception of play as a "new frontier" in the first place.

What does leisure space say about race, class, and gender issues?

As it turns out, quite a lot. The "leisure ethic" that emerged in the late nineteenth and early twentieth centuries was buttressed by often unspoken assumptions not only about racial and ethnic difference, but also about gender norms, socio-economic status, and thus also (perhaps ultimately) citizenship. A largely white, male, middle-class movement, play reform sought to recreate an America in its own image, drawing on new psycho-sociological theories about child development that stressed, for example, a "normal" evolution from the "primitive" to the "civilized" and a "natural" division of gender roles.

But this is also where discussions of work and play during this period get so interesting. In terms of gender, for example, the "less work, more play" mantra of the play reformers conflicted with the desires of many middle-class American women who were fighting for more meaningful work, not more capacious leisure. It's fascinating to see play theorists – and also corporate advertisers – try to redefine housework as a form of productive play. There's a wonderful series of articles in the popular early twentieth-century periodical, the *Outlook* (the TIME magazine of its day), titled "How to Make Play Out of Work," in which a home economist urges women to convert every day cleaning tasks into "glorious sport" that strengthens the body through gymnastic exercise and the spirit through competitive zeal. Who needs work outside the home when work inside the home can be so uplifting?

These prescriptions and redefinitions cut across lines of class and race as well. In *An American Tragedy*, for example,

65

Theodore Dreiser explores in almost numbing detail the ways that access to recreational opportunities – and quite literally the spaces of leisure – can be tightly regulated by social caste even in an era of comparative plenty. For working-class men and women of color, these constraints often multiply and can vary widely by place and region.

Which is not to say that possibilities didn't exist, even among such constraints, for the successful negotiation of satisfying work and play lives. One of the most intriguing things I discovered during my research was that Zora Neale Hurston once appeared in the recreation reform movement's national magazine (aptly titled *Recreation*) for her work with folk dances, songs, and games in the mid-1930s. And of all the writers in my study, it's Hurston who most clearly imagines a protagonist (Janie, in *In Their Eyes Were Watching God*) who achieves a measure of satisfying control over her labor and her leisure, even pointing – in ways the play reformers never quite conceived – to the potentially powerful efficacy of partnered work and partnered play.

In *Sites Unseen*, you assert that "it remains striking how persistently the imagery of 'Oriental' space in turn-of-the-century popular American literature rejects the very possibility that Americans might find themselves 'at home' either with, or within, Asian design." Tell us more about the "strategies of architectural racialization in popular American Orientalist narrative."

Popular American Orientalist narrative is obsessed with architectural and decorative otherness. Virtually every popular tale in the early twentieth century that depicts Asian characters, settings, or scenes, constructs racial difference in spatial terms. Think of the myriad representations of Chinatown in popular American fiction: narrow streets,

66

looming balconies, and violent colors above ground; trapdoors, hidden tunnels, and subterranean vaults (or sometimes, torture chambers) below. No other American racial or ethnic group is represented in quite this consistent a fashion. Sax Rohmer's *Fu Manchu* novels – with their dark cellars, luxurious carpets, and dragon tapestries – epitomize the genre. But even the less sensational stories of a writer like Frank Norris tend to embody the threat and allure of Asian-ness in vivid Chinatown streetscapes that simultaneously (and metonymically) entice and overpower.

What fascinated me in doing the research for this chapter in *Sites Unseen* was discovering how persistently these architectural and decorative tropes clung to popular narrative even as American architects – Frank Lloyd Wright, for example – openly embraced Asian design as part of a new American architectural aesthetic. Wright's integration of the simple horizontal lines, open floor plans, and natural settings common to Japanese domestic architecture in his famous Prairie Houses – design elements he first encountered in the Japanese Pavilion at the 1893 Chicago World's Fair – exists in jarring juxtaposition with stereotypical representations of "Oriental" buildings, objects, and décor in popular fiction.

Thus it was all the more surprising to me to find that Earl Derr Biggers's *Charlie Chan* novels – long derided for their stereotypical representations of racial character – did not foreground the architectural and decorative otherness so common to other popular texts of the period. In fact, Biggers's first novel, *The House Without a Key*, goes out of its way to interrogate the persistence of the Chinatown trope itself, displacing the tunnel and dungeon motifs of Rohmer with recurring images of outdoor gardens and spacious lanais – only to find the usual stereotypes thrusting back into view. I see Biggers using these sudden reappearances to ask why the

67

tropes are so difficult to shake off in the first place, theorizing, we might say – rather than merely rejecting – the architectural racialization so common to popular narrative.

Both *The Leisure Ethic* and *Sites Unseen* focus on issues concerning "spaces." How do you see the concepts connecting in regards to space between these two books?

This is a great question. Some people have asked me why these two books focus on such different topics. But as your question implies, for me they share a complementary interest in space, place, and narrative. I see both books, in other words, as part of the "spatial turn" in literary studies. *The Leisure Ethic*, in many respects, is a book about urban planning. It investigates the ideology behind the decisions to put playgrounds and parks in American cities, and then looks closely at those spaces themselves, in both actual and fictional settings. *Sites Unseen* moves from urban planning to architecture – from the streets to the buildings – and asks, in effect, "how does the built environment shape our experience of race?" and "what effect does race have on the ways that the interior and exterior spaces in which we live, work, and play shape us and the stories we tell?"

Both books have also been deeply shaped by the teaching I have done at Princeton for the Program in American Studies on culture, space, and society – most particularly a course called "American Places," which I've taught since the late 1990s, an interdisciplinary exploration of a broad range of spatial matters, including urban ecology, landscape and culture, race and the built environment, growth and sprawl, history and memory.

For you, space is invariably political.

Absolutely. One of the main arguments of *Sites Unseen* is that architectural design inevitably reflects and shapes deeply embedded ideas about access and power. Who belongs in which spaces, and at what times? What kinds of relationships do different architectural spaces make possible – or impossible? These are the kinds of questions with which *Sites Unseen* is centrally preoccupied. Indeed, all of the texts I study – from Hannah Crafts's *The Bondwoman's Narrative* and Charles Chesnutt's conjure tales, to Richard Harding Davis's *Three Gringos in Venezuela and Central America* and Olga Beatriz Torres's *Memorias de mi viaje (Recollections of My Trip)*, to Biggers's Charlie Chan novels – are intensely concerned with the politics of space.

M. THOMAS INGE

Professor M. Thomas Inge is the Robert Emory Blackwell Professor of Humanities at Randolph-Macon College. He is an authority on Southern literature and popular culture, especially comics, and has authored or edited over fifty books including the *Greenwood Guide to American Popular Culture* (2002); *Comics as Culture* (University Press of Mississippi 1999); *Anything Can Happen in a Comic Strip* (University Press of Mississippi, 1995); and *Charles M. Schulz: Conversations* (University Press of Mississippi, 2000). Professor Inge helped found the American Humor Studies Association and served as editor for *Studies in American Humor*.

I asked him about the scholarly study of humor.

You got your Ph.D. at Vanderbilt. Tell us about that time.

When I arrived at Vanderbilt in 1959, I had read little American literature, and I had no idea that the university had been the site of a major chapter in Southern and American literature. It was indeed the last days of the Fugitive and the Agrarian legacies, and I soon became aware of this as I took courses with Donald Davidson, John Crowe Ransom, and Walter Sullivan, and met or heard lectures by Allan Tate, Robert Penn Warren, Andrew Lytle, and the remaining living members of those movements. Most were kind and thoughtful people, and even though I was at the opposite end of the political spectrum on nearly all issues, I simply talked with them about literature rather than current events. I was fascinated with agrarianism as an idea and co-authored with a colleague two books about Donald Davidson and edited a textbook on *Agrarianism in American Literature*. From Davidson's course on folklore and the ballad, I learned that popular culture could be a more revealing reflector of society than traditional literature.

Who was your mentor during that time?

My mentor was Randall Stewart, the Hawthorne biographer and editor, then recently returned from Brown University to chair the English Department. He introduced me to George Washington Harris and his tales of Sut Lovingood, and from that engagement came an M.A. thesis, a Ph.D. dissertation, five books, and more than a dozen articles which have made a place for Harris in American literary history. This also opened up the world of humor which would lead to my involvement in establishing the American Humor Studies Association and a lifelong interest in teaching and writing about that most elusive of questions: what makes us laugh?

All of this led as well to an interest in Southern literature and culture and that most Southern of all writers, William Faulkner. But perhaps the pivotal moment came when a visiting writer, an aging but still beautiful and flirtatious Katherine Anne Porter, seductively looked me in the eye and then wrote in my copy of *The Leaning Tower and Other Stories*, quoting St. Augustine, "It doth make a difference whence cometh a man's joy." It was the literary life for me.

Talk to us more about the "opening up of the world of humor" for you – you are renowned for your scholarly work in the comic arts.

In high school, I had wanted to be a cartoonist, but I soon discovered that while I might make a competent one, I would never be a Walt Kelly, a Will Eisner, or a Milton Caniff. Most of the important things I had learned about life were from comic books and comic strips, and while I set aside my ambition to draw, I never gave up my love of the form.

After finishing my doctorate in English in 1964, my first job out was at Michigan State University in the Department of American Thought and Language, an interdisciplinary program. I quickly found myself reading more about American history, philosophy, economics, culture, and society than I had ever wanted to know. It became clear, however, that I was soon equipped to begin to make sense out of my fascination over the comics and to understand the powerful appeal of film and popular culture in general.

While I was at Michigan State, I was befriended by Russel Nye, who was then writing his groundbreaking study of popular culture *The Unembarrassed Muse*, and through him I became involved in the development of the popular culture movement. I would still rather draw and often say that I am a failed cartoonist who became a professor because I couldn't do any better.

You were the Resident Scholar in American Studies for the United States Information Service.

That was a dream job come true. I had already had three senior Fulbright lecturer grants to teach in Salamanca, Spain; Buenos Aires, Argentina; and Moscow, then the Soviet Union. I greatly enjoyed teaching abroad, so when I was offered the opportunity to become the Resident Scholar in American Studies at the U.S. Information Agency (not the CIA please note), now a part of the Department of State, I was set to go. My job was to do diplomatic work on behalf of encouraging students and teachers in other countries to study American history, literature, and culture. To study us is better to understand us I believed and still do. During the two years I held the position, I traveled and lectured in some twenty countries in Europe, Asia, and South America. One never knows what good diplomatic works does, but my efforts did lead to the development of some libraries, the assigning of some Fulbright lecturers, and the production of some exhibitions, as well as a large network of academic friends. I also edited a few textbooks that were used abroad for many years and received at least one citation for a successful project in Moscow. Whatever good I accomplished, however, I fear has been dismantled by the total collapse of American diplomacy and good will during the present administration.

Tell us about your experiences with the *Handbook of American Popular Culture* **and the** *Greenwood Guide to American Popular Culture*.

As the field of popular culture expanded almost overnight, and because it was brand new and had no methodology or theory to back it up, a lot of careless and superficial work was being turned out. One of the reasons for that was the lack of factual data and bibliographic material to support it. So I set out to provide some of that data and establish some publishing sites for sound and dependable scholarship.

The first *Handbook of American Popular Culture*, was meant to be just that, a "handbook," but it soon expanded into a three volume reference work, and then a four-volume revision, and finally the current four-volume *Greenwood Guide to American Popular Culture*, all well reviewed and pretty much accepted by the library and reference community as a standard work. Some feel it helped establish the parameters of the field of study, and it received an award from the American Library Association. A part of this program too was the beginning of a series of reference books and bio-bibliographies of figures in

73

popular culture for Greenwood Press, and a series of studies in popular culture with the University Press of Mississippi. All of this activity has been intended to help establish the legitimacy of popular culture in the academy.

You're most well known within the world of popular culture studies for your work on comics culminating in such books as *The American Comic Book*, *Comics in the Classroom*, *Comics as Culture*, *Great American Comics*, and *Anything Can Happen in a Comic Strip*. What do you see as your primary contributions to comics scholarship?

My intention has been to make it clear that the comic strips, comic books, and now graphic novels have always been as significant and important to our culture as all of the other arts, and that they contribute no less to the welfare and happiness of society than do film, painting, literature, drama, or music. Through my efforts and those of others, the comics are now an accepted field of study and teaching.

What more needs to be done in comics studies?

Lots of reprint editions of the classic comic strips, sound biographies of major artists, and scholarly studies and critical appreciations of figures, trends, and movements in comics history – all of which I am pleased to say are appearing on a regular basis from the university presses and commercial publishers.

MATTHEW FRYE JACOBSON

Matthew Frye Jacobson holds a Ph.D. in American Civilization from Brown University and serves as the William Robertson Coe Professor of American Studies and History at Yale University. His research interests revolve around race and the political culture of the United States over the last few centuries. He has written five books: *What Have They Built You to Do?: The Manchurian Candidate and Cold War America* (with Gaspar Gonzalez, University of Minnesota Press, 2006); *Roots Too: White Ethnic Revival in Post-Civil Rights America* (Harvard University Press, 2005); *Barbarian Virtues: The United States Encounters Foreign Peoples at Home and Abroad, 1876-1917* (Hill and Wang, 2000); *Whiteness of a Different Color: European Immigrants and the Alchemy of Race* (Harvard University Press, 1998); and *Special Sorrows: The Diasporic Imagination of Irish, Polish, and Jewish Immigrants in the United States* (University of California Press, 1995).

I asked him about his current work on his new book *Odetta's Voice and Other Weapons: The Civil Rights Era as Cultural History* and his work on the website Historian's Eye.

Tell us about your current project *Odetta's Voice and Other Weapons: The Civil Rights Era as Cultural History*. What is the purpose of your study?

This book started several years ago, when two smaller projects I was working on started to feel to me like different parts of the same big project. One was an essay on race and baseball that had been commissioned by Amy Bass for *In the Game*, a volume on race, identity, and sports; the other was an essay on music and social geography that evolved out of a lecture in my U.S. cultural history course at Yale.

The first piece focused on Dick Allen (baseball's iconic "bad boy" in the 1960s) and the rage that was unleashed upon him both by white fans and by the white press. (When Curt Flood refused to join the Phillies and launched his epic legal struggle against Major League Baseball for the right of free agency, it was in part because of the way Allen had been treated in Philadelphia.) I became interested in the diamond and the stadium as sites of racial struggle; I also became interested in Allen's story as so clearly a desegregation story, even though he came up fifteen years after Jackie Robinson had famously taken the field in Brooklyn.

The other article I was working on followed Jimi Hendrix from the integrated neighborhood of his native Seattle, through the segregated South during his years as a sideman on the chitlin' circuit, through a brief moment of artistic oblivion in New York (in mostly white bohemian clubs in the Village as well as mostly black blues clubs in Harlem), to his "discovery" by British rockers, his sudden fame in the UK, and his triumphal return to the U.S. at the Monterrey Pop Festival. I was interested in Hendrix's musical rearing in the African-American spaces of the rhythm and blues circuits, and in the peculiar racial cartography of his rise and of his fame. His is very much a story about race in popular musics – about the way it frames the general understanding of musical genre and that it organizes performance spaces, about the way it is obsessed over, misread, and contested. It is also a case study in social geography: in the U.S. he represented something of an oddity – a "black hippie" – while in the UK he represented "authenticity" itself, to the extent that he unnerved white performers ("imposters") like Clapton, Beck, and Townshend. This differential derives from the very different ways that whites in the U.S. and whites in the UK understood (or misunderstood) the relationship between rock and roll and African-American musical forms.

These two pieces gradually grew together and pointed me toward a set of larger issues: the relationship between Civil Rights history and various cultural forms, as a start; but more specifically, the significance of artistic expression as political expression (Odetta once said, "I could *sing* things that I could never *say*"), and the significance of audiences – or "taste publics" – as contending political publics. Cultural forms themselves were often sites of struggle, and consequently the culture industries became increasingly important to combatants on all sides. It's not just that a lot of black celebrities got involved in the movement or lent their names and their fame to the cause, for instance, but black celebrity itself in these years was always already politicized, if not by the artist (Odetta, Belafonte) then by the audience (Dick Allen).

The book that has grown out of these initial forays traces the arc of the Civil Rights Era, from the double V campaign of the 1940s to about the early 1970s, by focusing on a series of artists, entertainers, and cultural workers who were engaged in racial politics in wildly different ways. This study isn't meant to be exhaustive or comprehensive – it's not *a* cultural history, and it doesn't pretend to be. Rather it's a series of provocations – the era *as* cultural history – each chapter an occasion to think about a particular moment, a particular cultural form, and a particular political mood: Stump Cross (dance), Sammy Davis, Jr. (variety entertainment and popular autobiography), Odetta (folk music), Sidney Poitier (film), Diahann Carroll (television), Dick Gregory (stand-up comedy), Dick Allen (baseball), and Jimi Hendrix (rock). A brief epilogue looks at Blaxploitation and funk, and ponders

77

the "post" of the "post-Civil Rights Era."

What do you hope it contributes to scholarship on the Civil Rights Movement?

Well, there's been an explosion of really great scholarship in this area since I first began the project several years ago – especially in music and performance studies – and so the book maybe doesn't have to carry as much freight as I once thought it did. But I still think there is a lot to think through when it comes to the relationship between politics and performance, or in understanding the many cultural forms that had to be mobilized in order for the modern Civil Rights "public" to emerge.

You know, Odetta was an *archivist* in her musical practices; she put black history out there in the form of field hollers and work songs in a way that inspired African Americans and that challenged whites, and those coffee house settings in the late 1950s and early 1960s were really important to the formation of a politically engaged youth public. Diahann Carroll did battle with the network about how race and racism ought to be depicted at prime time – what was at stake ultimately was what she would be able to accomplish politically from the platform of her show *Julia*. We know a lot about the political significance of a figure like Paul Robeson, or Harry Belafonte maybe, but we don't know as much as we need to about the totality of that cultural history. So that's the first thing.

The second has more to do with the theoretical realm of inquiry. Not just recovering and fleshing out important examples of cultural figures accomplishing political work, but working to carry forward the theorizing of culture, race, and power. In this respect, each case is a little laboratory. Setting the analytical concepts of cultural studies in motion in this period – surrogation, hidden and public transcripts, fugitivity – tells us some things about both the national transformation and its limits in this era that we can't find out about by focusing on the major political figures like SNCC and King and Hamer and the Panthers.

Although you are concentrating on the Civil Rights Era, will the Obama presidency be mentioned?

I don't expect to write very much about Obama for this project, although I do end up spending a lot of time thinking about Obama and cultural history. The thing that strikes me – and I actually started thinking about this immediately, like *right* on election day – is that no one I know, of any generation or background or color, would have said in 2007 that the United States was about to elect an African-American president. Or ever would, maybe. But when Obama won, suddenly the decades between the Civil Rights Movement and 2008 looked different – there was something about the underground currents of American life that could not be seen or known until those election returns came in; but now you could look back across the 1990s, the 1980s, the 1970s and begin to ask new questions about the nature of social change.

This isn't to say that Obama's victory marked "the end of race" or of racism or any crazy thing like that, though there are certainly enough people who want to say so. The society is as stratified as ever – the problems, as persistent and intractable. Racist hiring and housing practices; skewed banking practices; mass incarceration and differentials in sentencing; police brutality. Not to mention the backlash we've seen against Obama anyway, even after we proved our "color blindness" by electing him – like Newt Gingrich's thinly coded trope of "the food stamp president." But nonetheless it is no small thing – it is positively *enormous* – that millions of

79

Americans paused and imagined a black president and then pulled the lever in his favor. From Jim Crow to *this*, how implausible.

This is where we need cultural history. This transformation is, in part, a political story, sure, involving a generation of African-American big-city mayors, the occasional national figure like Jesse Jackson or Colin Powell or even – ironically – Clarence Thomas or Condoleezza Rice; but I think in its most powerful dimensions it's a cultural story. You don't get from Nixon's Southern Strategy in 1968 to Obama's election in 2008 without the work that culture does. I mean this in the sense of Stuart Hall's dictum, "it is *culture* that outfits us to behave politically in certain ways and not in others." We can't explain Obama to ourselves – we can't really grapple with the subterranean changes taking place in the decades since Selma – without reference to figures like Toni Morrison, Bill Cosby, Michael Jordan, Oprah Winfrey, Derek Jeter, or Mariah Carey. Or Chris Rock. Or Tiger Woods. People who were speaking "race" in a different register than Carl B. Stokes, Shirley Chisholm, or Kurt Schmoke. People who in their work and in their public ubiquity were subtly changing minds – were outfitting people to behave differently.

Lastly, tell us about your website Historian's Eye.

This project began as an effort to document Obama's Inauguration Day itself, and at the outset that's all I thought it was going to be. I was working with a photographer named Renee Athay; we went to the Mall for the inauguration – we interviewed some folks on the train on the way down – and we spent the day photographing and interviewing people about the meaning that the day had for them and their understanding of what it meant for the country. And that was incredible. There was a kind of reverence for the moment that

80

hung in the air there that was really powerful. It was joyous, but also sober in a way. More church than party. And while we expected that the scale and the spectacle would be the most significant thing about the materials we gathered, actually the greatest historical power was carried in the individual voices and in individual faces.

Over the next several months I decided to keep going – to keep photographing and interviewing as a way of documenting this historical moment that kept getting more and more interesting. Depressing, too, but interesting. The thing that struck me then and that strikes me still is the feeling – shared among people I've spoken with across the political spectrum – that this is a unique moment of hope and despair. This feeling that, as a country, we could deliver up our very best or our very worst at any moment. This started with the fork in the road that was the 2008 election; but that feeling of hope and danger persists for most people. (Of course, one person's hope is another person's danger.)

So by now the project has evolved into a documentary website that houses over 2,500 photographs and about sixty interviews (audio and transcript) that cover the Obama presidency, the anti-Obama backlash, the economic collapse, the Tea Party, the wars, the anti-Muslim resurgence, the BP oil spill, the Occupy Movement, all within this general frame of the double-edgedness of the moment, hope and despair. It's meant as both an archive devoted to this extraordinary historical moment in the U.S., and as a pedagogical tool for thinking historically about the present – to think about the historical inventories we need to understand where we are, but also to think about the present as history-in-the-making. So it's meant for classroom use (and a lot of teachers and students are indeed using it), and there's also a participatory, "wiki" aspect to it, where people are invited to submit materials of their own to add to the archive. What does this historical moment look like where you live? Scores of people have submitted individual photographs, but some people have developed much more elaborate contributions: there's a whole gallery of photographs and interviews on the Tea Party, created by an ethnography student at NYU named A.J. Bauer; and right now there are groups at both NYU and Berkeley who are developing galleries on Occupy.

I haven't figured out how long this project goes on – just until it seems natural to stop, I guess. But there are days when it feels like I'm documenting the fall of the American Empire, and that this is probably what I'll be doing for the rest of my life.

E. ANN KAPLAN

E. Ann Kaplan is Professor of English and Comparative Literatures and founding Director of the Humanities Institute at the State University of New York, Stony Brook. In addition to producing countless lectures, journal articles, book reviews, and book chapters, Professor Kaplan has published no less than seven books (and edited or co-edited many others) including *Women and Film: Both Sides of the Camera* (Routledge, 1990); *Looking for the Other: Feminism, Film and the Imperial Gaze* (Routledge, 1997), and *Trauma Culture: The Politics of Terror and Loss in Media and Literature* (Rutgers, 2005).

I asked Professor Kaplan about the republication of *Motherhood and Representation: The Mother in Popular Culture and Melodrama*. Originally published in 1992, her seminal work was reprinted by Routledge in 2002.

You dedicate your book *Motherhood and Representation* to your daughter, Brett Kaplan, and your mother, Trudie Mercer. Tell us about them in relation to the project of this study.

I believe that all research is symptomatic. By which I mean that we choose topics because they have intrinsic meaning to us in addition to our wanting to make a scholarly contribution. I think the best research emerges when there is that intrinsic perhaps unconscious interest propelling us towards an area of study. This in no way affects the scholarly nature of the project, just the energy and drive behind the inquiry.

83

Giving birth in 1968, and before the second wave of the feminist movement was underway, I found myself up against many rigid concepts about what was, and what was not, "proper" to being a mother. I hardly dared tell my thesis director that I was pregnant, let alone the chair of the department where I was doing adjunct teaching. It was clear that being a working mother was not the norm. When I got divorced a couple of years later, I realized that it was even worse to be a single working mother.

The idea for the book arose out of these multiple experiences and concerns. I wanted to know more about the history of motherhood as a set of discourses, and since I was a film scholar, about images and narratives of mothering. I wanted to know how it was that in the imaginary of Western cultures women were divided into "virginal" or saintly mothers and somewhat scorned sexual beings, in a situation where never the twain should meet. Mothers could not be sexual it seemed; sexual women could not be mothers. Where did this all arise in mainstream U.S. culture? Why were these old ideas retained in popular culture? How far had the ideas been produced by (largely but not exclusively) male psychologists and psychoanalysts? How far were any of the discourses based in unavoidable biological "givens"? How far did discourse take advantage of biology?

You bring an openness and an honesty to your text, uncommon in academic writing. For example, in your preface you write, "I could not combine sex, work and motherhood during all those years we lived together without any kind of 'third' to provide a cushion or to usefully intervene in the dyad." Why did you decide to write in this style?

The "openness" and autobiographical comments are only to be found explicitly in the preface. After that, I return to the usual academic and scholarly discourse, although, as noted above, the intensity of my ideas and the passion one can perhaps sense behind the prose comes from what I say in the preface. I don't recall actively making a "choice" about being open. I think I wanted my mother and my daughter to know in a public way what they meant to me. Moreover, I wanted them to know that my relations with them were an intrinsic part of the intellectual life that had taken me away from them. I especially wanted my daughter to know this, since she suffered the most from my being a single mother, living far from my family, given the prevailing discourses and institutions of the time. Few of my female colleagues had children; there was very little tolerance of children in the workplace; there were few appropriate or available daycare centers, and even fewer within my meager financial resources.

It seemed important to put in print that women scholars' lives cannot so easily be divided into teaching and research on the one hand, family on the other. Male scholars perhaps could do this since at least at that time, they had their wives as homemakers. For working women, things were intertwined and far more complicated.

Your book was first published in 1992 then reprinted in 2002. Do you have any thoughts about the decision to reprint it?

In regard to the reprinting of *Motherhood*, I was not consulted. Had I known, I would have suggested writing a new preface, no doubt containing some of my thoughts articulated for this interview. I believe the book was ahead of its time. Interest in motherhood from a critical feminist standpoint was only just starting. I assume that the publishers recognized the ongoing interest in motherhood and saw that my book still spoke to that interest in useful ways. For which I am grateful, of course!

Before the second wave feminist movement, psychology and psychoanalytic scholars had continued to research and write about mothers, but mainly from traditional standpoints. Pioneering 1970s books by Jane Lazarre, Dorothy Dinnerstein, and Adrienne Rich had started a critical exploration from contemporary feminist viewpoints when I decided to examine images in film and popular culture with a brief look back at the history of mothering discourses and at select literary representations.

The decision to reprint was most likely the result of recent discussions in the popular press about many career women's decisions to quit working or drastically reduce their career ambitions in order to spend time with their babies. The discourse comes upon the heels of a period (roughly 1995 to 2003) when it was (more or less) taken for granted that middle-class mothers would continue to work – whereas working class women had always had to do so. Daycare centers, while still not abundant, had proliferated. If their cost was often prohibitive, middle-class women were still using them or finding other solutions.

The decision of a high profile government administrator in the Clinton era to leave her post to be with her children sparked a response in many career women enduring a similar sort of split between wishing to have more time for their children and demands of the office. While my book looks back to an earlier period, the questions it raises about the tension for women between personal fulfillment in intellectual or other kinds of work and fulfillment in raising children perhaps apply to more

86

women than ever today since more middle-class women have entered the workforce.

What drew you toward melodrama?

Since I am a film and literary scholar and my project was about images of the mother, I chose the literary and film genres that focused on maternity and the domestic sphere. Thus, the so-called sentimental women's novel, theatre, and film melodrama had to be central in the work. In the major film genres – the western, the gangster film, film noir, the war film, epics – others rarely figured and, if they did, they were in minor roles. Partly because the sentimental novel and the melodrama focused on mothers and women's home lives, these genres were traditionally scorned by the male literary and film establishment.

When I studied select texts in these genres, I found that they varied in terms of the position the text seemed to adopt in relation to the mother and the domestic sphere to which she was traditionally limited. Some texts accepted that the mother was a figure necessarily subservient to a dominant patriarchal order although the narrative positioned itself within the mother's point of view and showed her suffering and often unjust treatment (*East Lynne* was a classic example of such a text; *Stella Dallas* a more complex one with later versions). Other texts offered stories that challenged female and maternal subservience, and showed mothers achieving independence, having sex outside of marriage, and finding enough autonomy to leave home, even. I called these the "resisting" texts to indicate that they questioned ruling discursive norms.

Talk to us about the mother-paradigm shift in relation to postmodernism.

87

In regard to the U.S. (and Eurocentric) cultures, I distinguished three predominant mother paradigms which evolved during the eighteenth and nineteenth centuries along with the industrial revolution and bourgeois culture – those of the angel in the house (saintly, self-sacrificing mother); the over-indulgent, over-protective mother; and the phallic or evil one, who is jealous of or tries to harm her children. I focused on these paradigms because they form an historical background against which to observe contemporary motherhood discourses. Postmodern theories introducing the concept of flexible identities did indeed enable me to conceptualize women in the late twentieth century as having multiple non-essentialized identities. Instead of being locked into the fixed identities – sex object, mother (in its three forms), blue-stocking, mistress, etc. – women are seen to occupy many different positions and subjectivities. Before, the fixed identities were ones imposed by patriarchal culture. Woman was sex object, not a subject of sexuality; her roles were conceptualized from the perspective of patriarchy and its needs.

Postmodernism together with feminism opened up new possibilities and new ways of thinking about women. How far in any specific context women are able to mobilize and make use of these new possibilities is another question. But western women at least now conceive of themselves as having multiple roles, of which being a mother is only one, and in regard to which the earlier paradigms barely apply. It may be the most important or insistent identity until children are grown up. But whether as choice or necessity, most women are now combining motherhood with some kind of work or other pursuits or interests during child-rearing years.

You do not discuss the fourth mother, the "real life"

mother. You "believe she is ultimately non-representable as such," yet she is "enormously important" to you.

What I had in mind here is that the infinite variety of individual, specifically located mothers are impossible to write about with any authority. There is simply too much variety in the ways women experience and perform motherhood for any discussion to encompass all practices, or to take account of how class and cultural differences affect mothering. But I am arguing that we can locate and discuss pervasive social mothering discourses, including images of and narratives about mothers. While not every woman adheres to the norms these discourses lay out, each mother in any specific historical moment has to deal with, or adjust to them. The discourses provide a terrain within which she must learn to mother. Her behaviors may not be that much affected (although surely to an extent they will be), but she may worry that she is not doing the right thing, that she is failing somehow to live up to a norm, she may struggle with internal feelings opposite to the norms, and in this way her mothering is impacted upon.

Robert Mitchell's 2004 film *The Mother* provides a good example of a mother who had to struggle against her own disinclination to mother in a culture where she was supposed to stay home and enjoy this role. This is what I had in mind when I said that "women, like everyone else, can function only within the linguistic, semiotic constraints of their historical moment." I would not put it quite so starkly now. It's more that women have to deal with whatever constraints (including political and social ones) apply in any particular historical moment. They can depart to a degree, but still they know about the constraints and have to decide how far they can endure departing from norms.

89

The Mother addresses many a taboo subject.

Yes, Mitchell's film (made from a script by Hanif Kureishi) addresses aspects of motherhood still rarely dealt with in cinema. The film focuses on a middle-aged mother, apparently not close to her grown-up children or her grandchildren, who arrives at her children's London homes when her husband suddenly dies. One theme deals with the complexities of the mother's relationship to her daughter, who feels the mother never gave her affection and never encouraged her in her artistic pursuits. It turns out that indeed the mother was not drawn to mothering and struggled with guilt about this. But a major theme is the mother's newfound interest in sex. The most dramatic episodes involve the middle-aged mother's sexual awakening when she is attracted to her daughter's boyfriend. The film dares to breach several cultural taboos: that of motherhood and sexuality; of middle-aged sexual passion; and of a mother taking a child's lover for herself. The film does not judge the mother, although it does not necessarily support what she does. Rather, it opens up questions for spectators to think about in a historical moment when such questions become possible.

In earlier times, mothering discourses were such that a mass media work introducing issues such as these would rarely have gotten financial backing. Only one text in my book, a very early one at that, dares to approach the issue of motherhood and sexuality in any way other than totally blaming the mother, and that is Herbert Brennan's 1926 *Dancing Mothers* (interestingly, this is a film in which the mother also takes her daughter's lover, only in this case without knowing that the man is involved with her daughter). While we have moved away from the paradigms noted above to the extent that they no longer determine the only possibilities for mother figures, these images lurk behind

90

much contemporary discussion of motherhood. I believe they partly account for the new books arguing for the pleasures of staying home instead of trying to have a career along with mothering. The rationale is now different of course: Women are saying that this is what they choose to do, not what is forced upon them. And that is a big shift. Yet I wonder how far that is really the case. Would such women make this choice if society made it more possible to combine work and motherhood by having high quality, state-funded child care in the workplace, for example? Or by having flexible hours for office and factory workers at all levels? Or really integrating men into child rearing, even more than the new fathers today are integrated? And old paradigms may be seen in the fact that women who may not want to mother are still viewed critically, or as somehow "lacking" if they make this choice.

Psychoanalytic theory is integral to your argument.

Some of the pioneering books on motherhood by feminists combined a psychoanalytic and sociological approach. As already noted, I was inspired by the work of Adrienne Rich, Jane Lazarre, and Dorothy Dinnerstein, all of whom brought feminist ideas to thinking about motherhood, and included psychological aspects. Of these writers, though, only Dorothy Dinnerstein used a psychoanalytic approach (Object Relations, in her case) as such, and none of them dealt with cinema in depth.

It seemed to me impossible to understand motherhood and mother-child relations without using psychoanalysis. Much in regard to individual behavior and feelings and to collective discourses about motherhood has to do with unconscious traces of issues between children and mothers. My approach was perhaps unusual in combining elements of Object Relations psychoanalytic theory (this originated with Freud but was developed by Melanie Klein and Donald Winnicott) with elements of French Lacanian theories as taken up by French feminists.

Lacan's concept of there being two related psychic registers – that of the Imaginary and of the Symbolic – was useful in differentiating the individual's unconscious fantasy or idealized mother figure from the social category of the mother set up by patriarchy. I used this schema somewhat reductively, but it referred to an abstract cultural system which subjects participated in without full awareness. The scheme was particularly useful for analyzing images of the mother in popular culture – the main topic of my book – since cinema as a cultural form automatically reproduced these imaginary and symbolic mother constructs. Films about mother-child relations were extremely fruitful for pointing out ways western culture thought about, and positioned, the mother.

Winnicott and other Object Relations theorists like Daniel Stern, on the other hand, were useful for thinking about lived mother-child relations. While this was not a main topic of the book, it was hard to limit myself only to cinematic images when I had been inspired by my own experiences as a mother to write the book in the first place. In any case, it is hard for any subjects to keep separate the realm of lived reality from that of fantasy and of images that surround us in culture. It seemed to me that what film images did not show was the ways in which the child needs a holding environment between the shock of being born unprepared into the world and becoming a subject in that world. A loving, caring figure is needed as the child struggles to come to terms with, and learn to know, objects as distinct from herself. But this figure does not have to be the biological mother! In earlier eras, rich families hired nannies to undertake this position. In our day, increasingly, it's the father or grandmother who provides the holding environment. Or mothers share the role with such family members.

Men, particularly Darwin, Rousseau, and Marx, affect motherhood discourse as well.

From time to time, a thinker comes along who latches onto subtle cultural shifts in norms and ways of being before anyone has had time to realize any shift was taking place. The thinker sets about theorizing the shift, and because in a sense cultures were unconsciously preparing for it, the thinker's work hits a nerve, arouses discussion, and often then contributes to the shift taking place. All three thinkers noted here are of this type. Of course, Freud is as well, but I have discussed his centrality to my project already. Darwin's ideas of the survival of the fittest – misapplied and taken out of context when popularized – gave rise to the nineteenth-century (now discredited) eugenics movement, putting pressure on middle-class women to have children and refuse birth control (including abortion) in order to prevent deterioration of the human species by the greater reproductive activity of the poor. Rousseau's *Emile* marks the shift to a new idea of the child as a subject in its own right, and as requiring particular care and attention along with specific education in morality and citizenship if democracy is to succeed. Rousseau's insight was crucial for Freud's work, of course, and for western culture's ongoing interest in and absorption with the child, but unfortunately it also had the effect of putting the burden of caring for the child on the mother. So, just as the child gets newly constituted by Rousseau, so does the mother. This has some positive aspects for her as well – it makes her important and gives her social responsibility. But it locks her into the domestic sphere, at least in bourgeois families.

93

And this is where Marx comes in. That is, Marx provides a class analysis for thinking about mothering, and this was a focus I could not develop within the parameters of the book, although I deal at length with working class and minority mothers in select films, like *Stella Dallas* (1937), and both versions of *Imitation of Life*. I note at the outset that for coherence and because of the importance of bourgeois culture in modern industrializing nations, and finally because the most popular works dealt with middle-class society, I look mainly at the bourgeois mother. However, King Vidor's *Stella Dallas*, about a working class mother, demonstrates points just made in that Stella believes her child will be better off under the care of the upper middle-class mother than under her own working class care.

You close your book by stating, "For women, one of the most subordinated and fetishized positions has been that of 'mother.' Once this position is opened up as only a part of any specific woman's subjectivity, not the all-consuming entirety of it; once any specific woman is seen to be constituted 'mother' only when interacting with her child; once 'mother' is no longer a fixed, essentialized quality, then women may be freed from the kind of discursive constraints and burdens studied in this book." Has this change begun? Have books like yours made a difference?

Hearing that quotation from my book, I realize just how much has changed since I started my book! I had only to recall my own difficult experiences being a mother and a full-time professor and to compare my situation with that of my daughter, now also a full-time professor with two very young children, to see that the mother position is now indeed no longer taken as the all-consuming identity it still was in the mid 1960s. My daughter is apparently freed from the discursive motherhood constraints and burdens that I studied

94

in the book. Most of her many female colleagues have children and juggle work and mothering without discursive burdens. The literal burdens of women having many roles is something else. But even here things have changed drastically in that all the young fathers now share as much as they can in the work of raising children. The children are seen as the equal responsibility of both parents, and this has been an eye-opener for me.

From the start, my son-in-law took a major responsibility for changing diapers, dressing and feeding the babies, playing with them, going to the doctor etc. The new 1980s images of the nurturing father I talk about in the book finally also had a social reality in the millennium. I am sure there are still many families in which the burden for childcare still falls on the mother for all kinds of reasons. Many lower class women are single working mothers, with very few options. But what has changed is the expectation that fathers will share in all aspects of child rearing. The father role has been opened up to include "mothering," as it were.

Books like mine have certainly made a difference, but the Women's Liberation Movement and various following feminist movements have done the brunt of the work of opening up the mother position. Women's Studies classes have no doubt also had a big impact on raising the consciousness of new generations of women in regard to opening out female identities beyond marriage and motherhood. The United States economy, and the need (as well as the desire in many cases) for most middle class as well as working class women to work if couples are to live in the lifestyle they want, or just to put food on the table, has changed motherhood discourse as well.

95

Would you like to make any changes or additions to the text now?

When I wrote this book, I had planned a follow-up volume that would deal with multicultural mothers. I highlighted my difficult decision to trace discourses in regard largely to white middle class women, noting that middle class motherhood discourse, as is so often the case, put pressure on other women (whether of different ethnicity or class) to follow suit. Or, to put this better: These dominant discourses often position people unable to fit the picture as somehow "lacking." The tendency is to strive for what the dominant dictates. Thus, knowing this white middle class mothering discourse and its histories, I thought would provide a starting point for studying multicultural women and their dilemmas or attitudes towards mothering. Unfortunately, as so often in my work, I took a sort of sideways path to fulfilling the project instead of confronting it head on. My next book, *Looking for the Other: Feminism, Film and the Imperial Gaze*, does look at mother-daughter relations as imaged in films by multicultural women but the context is much broader than the earlier volume, namely postcolonial studies and oppressive images of ethnic "others" in general. As I write, some of my students are working on images of motherhood and ethnicity in literature. I may return to this lapsed project in the future. In addition, increasing visibility is being given to gay couples who are parents. While issues already mentioned are no doubt pertinent to these couples as well, other specific concerns may need study.

But aside from dealing with groups neglected in the book, I would need now to deal with the very different "culture" in the U.S. surrounding motherhood, some of it good, some questionable. To begin with, as I said, it's now assumed by new parents today that the husband will play, if not quite an

96

equal, at least a highly involved role with the children. Secondly, it seems that the concept of the "child-centered" family is now being taken to extremes. Many parents make the child the focus of attention and set all adult routines of eating and sleeping in accord with the child's routines. But it's more than that: it's that thinking about the child governs everything while the child is awake in ways that did not happen earlier. It may be that this "child-centered" home is a function of the fact that for much of the day both parents are at work, and the child is in day care. Thus, the home time becomes child time. This makes a certain amount of sense. But I wonder how far the child-centered concept enters into families when one of the parents is not working? Are those families less child-centered in this way? It would be good to know. What is clear is a new interest in mothers taking pleasure in their children, and either staying home with them, if they can afford it, or drastically cutting back on career aims in order to watch their children grow up.

GEORGE LIPSITZ

George Lipsitz, Professor of American Studies and Black Studies at the University of California, Santa Barbara, has authored many books, including *The Possessive Investment in Whiteness* (Temple University Press, 1988); *Rainbow at Midnight: Life and Labor in the 1940s* (University of Illinois Press, 1994); *A Life in the Struggle: Ivory Perry and the Culture of Opposition* (Temple University Press, 1995); *Dangerous Crossroads: The Sidewalks of St. Louis* (Verso, 1997); as well as *Time Passages: Collective Memory and American Popular Culture* (University of Minnesota Press, 2001). His awards include the Eugene M. Kayden Press Book Award, the Gustavus Myers Outstanding Book Award, and the Anisfield-Wolf Book Award.

Professor Lipsitz is virtually a father of Americana: The Institute for the Study of American Popular Culture and this journal. Although he is not associated with us in any formal sense, his seminal essay "Listening to Learn and Learning to Listen: Popular Culture, Cultural Theory, and American Studies," published in *American Quarterly* (1990) and reprinted in *Locating American Studies: The Evolution of a Discipline* (1999) made us aware of the need to form an institute and publish a journal dedicated to the art of listening to American popular culture because here we would find the "voices" that write, play, film, photograph, manufacture, tell, dance, sculpt, paint, and thus explain our American story, our American history.

I caught up with Professor Lipsitz to ask him about his career, the state of American popular culture studies, and his now famous essay.

How did you first get interested in the study of American popular culture?

Some years ago, a reporter from *Musician* magazine asked jazz pianist Abdullah Ibrahim a similar question about when his interest in music began. Ibrahim said he understood the logic of the question, but that he couldn't answer it, because music had always been part of his day to day living. I feel the same way about my relationship to popular culture. I can't remember a time when I didn't have a deep investment in music, in sports, in story-telling of all kinds.

In recent years, I have come to understand more clearly how these investments were shaped. My parents grew up in the 1920s and 1930s. As children of working class immigrant parents, they viewed education, ideas, and culture with reverence. All the humiliation and subordination that they and their parents faced for being foreigners, for being Jews, for being working class conflicted with the self-esteem and self-respect they felt for themselves and for their community. The public schools offered them an opportunity to demonstrate their merit, to display their talents and abilities, to prove that they could master all the prestigious cultural forms that were considered the private preserve of more privileged groups. They read the great books, listened to classical music, and became knowledgeable about sculpture and painting. This created in them a disposition against popular culture, a fear that common tastes might make them appear undiscerning and unworthy. At the same time, they listened and danced to swing music, loved motion pictures, and played and followed sports. The celebratory "America" of the New Deal "cultural front" turned immigrants and their children from unwanted aliens into redemptive insiders. Like millions of other ethnic Americans, my parents secured a measure of cultural and political inclusion for themselves through the populism and

99

celebrations of regional and ethnic specificity that fueled the New Deal "culture of unity." Yet the years after World War II transformed popular culture in important ways. The enormous expansion of consumer spending, the rise of new communications media, and the incorporation of distinct European American ethnic cultures and communities into a more generalized white identity left me with a different view of culture than the one that made sense to my parents. Like Jim Burden in Willa Cather's *My Antonia*, the comfortable middle class home, community, and culture in which I grew up felt like a kind of suffocating tyranny to me. I was drawn to rhythm and blues radio programs, country and western songs, film noir movies, and the hard scrabble world I imagined that professional athletes inhabited. It was my way of re-enacting the popular front – of leaving behind my ethnic name and the teasing and bullying it seemed to provoke – my losing myself in an "America" defined by the exotic hometowns of baseball players printed on the backs of baseball cards, by the "down home" humor of disc jockeys, and by the ferocious theatricality, aggressive festivity, and sensuality of mass mediated working class culture. It was also a way of dissenting from the assimilation my parents fought so hard to secure, to invert the hierarchies of U.S. society and find truths in its more desperate and neglected precincts.

What first made you think American popular culture was important enough for academic study? In other words, whats so important about American popular culture?

I never intended to be a scholar of popular culture. In the early 1970s, I was part of a radical collective that concentrated our efforts by supporting an oppositional rank and file caucus in Teamsters Local 688 in St. Louis. When we were totally and completely defeated, I enrolled in graduate school hoping to learn enough about labor history to understand our failure.

100

Yet the methods of labor history at that time were better suited to discovering the history of labor's institutions than of workers themselves. I turned to popular culture as part of a worldwide movement by activists, intellectuals, and scholars to replace "labor history" with "workers history." Workers left very little in the way of archival evidence about the past, but working class culture turned out for me to provide the key to understanding the "strategies of independence" that fueled the mass strikes of the 1940s and shaped subsequent working class cultures of opposition, including the one I encountered in St. Louis.

Those studies taught me that many scholars had already studied culture in that way – European scholars Stuart Hall, Antonio Gramsci, Mikhail Bakhtin, but also those working in "the other American Studies tradition"—Toni Cade Bambara, C.L.R. James, Americo Paredes, Le Roi Jones, Leslie Marmon Silko, Johnny Otis, Horace Tapscott, Robert Warshow, and John Okada, among others.

Was there any specific catalyst for writing "Listening to Learn, Learning to Listen: Popular Culture, Cultural Theory, and American Studies"?

My conscious intention was to encourage scholars in American Studies to use our disagreements with each other in more productive ways. I think that our work is so difficult that we can't afford to avoid any methods or theory that might help us. I think that if you want other people to see the truth in what you are writing, you have to recognize the truth in their work. You may not like what they have to say, but there is a reason for it. I think we can learn from everybody. But we don't act like we can. We engage in Oedipal battles against the oldest or newest paradigms. We ridicule work we don't understand. We confuse disagreements over methods and

101

theories with moral worth. In writing "Listening to Learn," I was attempting to prevent unnecessary ruptures within American Studies. I was hearing a great deal of hostility in the field against cultural studies from scholars trained in the myth-image-symbol school, and equally harsh (and unfounded) attacks on post-structuralism and other kinds of "European" cultural theory by scholars trained in the myth-image-symbol and social science traditions. Cultural studies scholars and post-structuralists did not appreciate adequately the accomplishments of previous paradigms – the spaces they opened up under difficult conditions. I thought these arguments obscured the value of cultural theory in general, but also obscured the rich critical traditions in American studies that had not named themselves as theoretical schools. I felt that I had learned things of value from all of these traditions. I didn't see why we couldn't have it all – Alan Trachtenberg and Stuart Hall, Leo Marx and Jacques Derrida, Janice Radway and Henry Nash Smith, Celia Cruz and Gilles Deleuze, Jacques Lacan and Chaka Khan.

In "Listening to Learn," you noted that we need not fear European cultural theory (and that American Studies even seemed to anticipate many of its moves). Have you seen that theory integrated into American Studies in ways you would deem positive since 1990? Or have you seen Americanists veer way from it? In other words, what are your thoughts on European cultural theory?

I think that American Studies at its best produces a sophisticated blend of empirical and theoretical approaches to cultural questions. The work that has been produced in the past decade has been exemplary in that respect. Look at the grounded uses of theory that permeate the writings of senior scholars like Robin Kelley, Janice Radway, Dana Nelson, Chela Sandoval, Rosa Linda Fregoso, and Herman Gray.

102

Look at the first books produced by American Studies scholars in the 1990s – Tricia Rose's *Black Noise,* Rob Walser's *Running with the Devil*, Jenifer Devere *Brody's Impossible Purities*, Farah Jasmine Griffin's *Who Set You Flowin'*, George Sanchez's *Becoming Mexican American*, Lizabeth Cohen's *Making a New Deal*, Lynn Spigel's *Make Room for TV*. Look at the extraordinary work in American Studies being conducted by social scientists, by Arlene Davila in *Latinos, Inc.*, Claire Jean Kim in *Bitter Fruit*, Pierette Hondagneu-Sotelo in *Gendered Transitions*, Rick Bonus in *Locating Filipino Americana*. Look at the books that have been thrown forth in the past few years as the first publications by a new generation of scholars: Helena Simonett's *Banda*, Nayan Shah's *Contagious Divides*, Susan Phillips's *Wallbangin'*, Rachel Buff's *Immigration and the Political Economy of Home*, Joe Austin's *Takin' the Train*, Matt Garcia's *A World of Their Own*, and Melani McAlister's *Epic Encounters*. This wonderful work has more than fulfilled the promise we hoped for in 1990.

While you do allow for some use of European cultural theory, you also warn against being consumed by it. Indeed, in "Listening to Learn," you argued, "In my view, American Studies would be served best by a theory that refuses hypostatization into a method, that grounds itself in the study of concrete cultural practices, that extends the definition of culture to the broadest possible contexts of cultural production and reception, that recognizes the role played by national histories and traditions in cultural contestation, and that understands that struggles over meaning are inevitably struggles over resources." Have you seen your call come to fruition?

I think that the cultural criticism carried on by artists in recent years has been ahead of the cultural criticism carried on by scholars. Horace Tapscott's posthumously published memoir *Songs of the Unsung* is one of the most important books ever written. The poetry and spoken word art of Marisela Norte, Roberta Hill, Luis Alfaro, and Elizabeth Alexander (among others) has been amazing. But young scholars attuned to this work have played an important role in its development through their critiques, compliments, and all around championing of community artists who make an art out of talking back. I greatly admire what Michelle Habell-Pallan has done for a broad range of Latina cultural creators, how Tricia Rose has influenced women in hip hop, how Josh Kun's scholarship and journalism so brilliantly focuses attention on the new art emerging all around us.

In "Listening to Learn," you urge scholars to consider such popular culture artifacts as the Lindy-hop, Rupert Murdoch, and the Angry Samoans; "we neglect them only at our peril," you note. We take it from your previous comments that you have seen scholars pay more attention to such modes of popular culture? The field is no longer dominated by research on such figures as Ralph Ellison and on such themes as the popular detective fiction of Chester Himes?

It is not easy to look at popular culture both from close-up and far away. But scholars who have some love and respect for the people they study have produced wonderful work explaining how popular culture enables people to make meaning for themselves under circumstances they do not control. Ruby Tapia's research on photojournalism and racialized motherhood, Brenda Bright's work on low riders, Lilia Fernandez's studies of house music, Michael Eric Dyson's interventions in hip hop, Ryan Moore's study of white youths involved in punk rock, Michael Willard's examination of skate-boarding, Sarah Banet-Weiser's

104

explorations into beauty pageants come to mind. Historians have been particularly successful in studying commercial culture. Nan Enstad's *Ladies of Labor* is an extraordinary study of the intersections between popular fiction and fashion for working women in the 1920s. Linda Maram's explorations into Filipino participation in boxing and taxi dance halls are superb.

In the essay, you note that university budgets shape the research being done. At one point, you assert, "[S]truggles over meaning are also struggles over resources. They arbitrate what is permitted and what is forbidden; they help determine who will be included and who will be excluded; they influence who gets to speak and who gets silenced." How do you see the university structure and budget as shaping American popular culture studies now, some years later?

I think we are headed toward a two-tiered system of education and a two-tiered system of mass communication. Segregation by race and class makes it very difficult for people to see the things that connect them to or divide them from other people. As universities increasingly train a small elite and absorb the indirect costs of research and production for corporations, cultural studies runs the risk of becoming the research and development arm of the advertising industry. We have to do as much as we can inside the universities, but we have to reach outside them and connect with the communities and cultures that feel most deeply the oppressive, unequal, and unjust nature of our society.

Were you disappointed that as late as 1990 American Studies still needed to hear the message you delivered in "Listening to Learn"?

105

Like any of us, I could spend all day talking about what I think is wrong with our field, our work, our personalities, our ethics, our morals, our citizenship, our scholarship, and our teaching. It hurts to see us squander the resources we have and the mission that has been entrusted to us as a result of our privilege – our ability to speak and be heard in many different venues. We have the same contradictions as anybody else in this society, the same selfishness, sexism, competitiveness, greed, heartlessness, and cruelty. But the things we are doing wrong are still less impressive to me than what we are doing that is right. The tide can't be pushed back. Our times have generated a generation of intellectuals, artists, and activists who know what time it is. They know what to do, why, and when. We're all lucky to be part of this moment.

What is the future of American popular culture studies?

The only person I know who thinks he or she can predict the future is Lee "Hacksaw" Hamilton, a San Diego sportscaster. His predictions about who is going to win forthcoming football games are made so confidently, you wonder why they even bother to play the games. And of course, I show a lot of deference to anyone whose parents named him "Hacksaw." He probably has brothers and sisters named Ripsaw, Chainsaw, and Jigsaw. But the truth is, Hacksaw rarely gets it right. The future holds surprises that we can't anticipate. All in all, we'd rather have it that way. The challenge is not to know what the future will bring, but to be ready for the things it will demand of us. Count Basie's great drummer Jo Jones once said his job was not so much to play the drums as it was to get himself into the kind of condition where he could play the things he could imagine. I think that's our job too.

What would you call for now in the field of American popular culture studies? Is there a current crisis like the

106

one you noted in 1990?

We have to rethink the links that connect the nation, the citizen subject, sexuality, desire, and consumption. The work of Rod Ferguson, M. Jacqui Alexander, Ruby Tapia, Nayan Shah, Judith Halberstam, and many others are pointing us in that direction and helping us understand what we need to know.

CARMEN R. LUGO-LUGO

Carmen R. Lugo-Lugo is an Associate Professor in the Department of Critical Culture, Gender, and Race Studies at Washington State University where she also received her Ph.D. Her research and teaching interests include Puerto Rican and Latina/o Studies, Latina feminism in the U.S., popular culture and issues of race and gender, literature and issues of race/ethnicity and gender, feminist theory, colonialism/ imperialism, and race relations.

She has published many book chapters and articles. Her books include *A New Kind of Containment: "The War on Terror," Sexuality, and Race* (Rodopi Press, 2009) with Mary K. Bloodsworth-Lugo; *Containing (un)American Bodies: Race, Sexuality, and Post-11 September 2001 Constructions of Citizenship* (Rodopi Press, 2010) with Mary K. Bloodsworth-Lugo; *Animating Difference: Race, Gender, and Sexuality in Contemporary Films for Children* (Rowman & Littlefield, 2010) with C.R. King and Mary K. Bloodsworth; and *Productions of Race, Gender, and Citizenship in Recent Hollywood Films* (Rowman & Littlefield, 2014) also with Mary K. Bloodsworth.

I asked her about her work in popular culture, gender, race, and American Studies.

You hold a Ph.D. in American Studies from Washington State University. What drew you to that field?

What drew me was the possibility of doing research beyond disciplinary boundaries. Both my B.A. [University of Puerto

108

Rico] and my M.A. [University of Washington] are in sociology (a discipline that still fascinates me), and although I felt relatively comfortable doing sociology, I always felt constrained by its theoretical and methodological limits – which, to be fair, are actually imposed by sociologists and not necessarily by the discipline itself.

American Studies allowed me to research what I wanted to study using transdisciplinary theories and methodologies, a much richer approach, in my view. In American Studies, nobody frowns at my data sources or at my mixture of theories. Thus, I can work on developing an analysis of the MTV Music Awards by watching the show or an analysis of President Bush's rhetoric by using newspaper articles and nobody blinks. Similarly, I can use Hardt and Negri's theories of the multitude and empire and mix them with Chomsky's idea of the public, and that's fine. Of course, I don't mean to say that American Studies provides a free-for-all deal. Regardless of the area of research or discipline, academic research requires certain standards and adheres to certain methodological principles. But in a transdisciplinary field such as American Studies (Ethnic Studies and Women Studies are two other examples), there is a certain freedom of movement, a fluidity that was not available to me in sociology.

Speaking of the MTV Music Awards, you continue to show an interest in popular culture studies especially in terms of race and gender.

I agree with Noam Chomsky when he argues that media (though I would add popular culture as a whole) is a source of propaganda for any government and a significant way of manufacturing consent among the public. More importantly, popular culture is an unchecked tool that teaches the masses how to behave in relation to those in power. Thus, popular culture serves as an agent (and at times as a "whipping boy") for the political and economic interests of the elite (or those "in charge"). I became interested in popular culture because of its troubling role as a shaper of ideologies and a creator of approval and because of the way it informs and maintains the troubling relationship between the elite and the masses. In essence, I wanted to understand and analyze the processes by which popular culture teaches us all "who" to be.

Another thing that drew me to the study of popular culture was the criticism I saw leveled at those studying it. They were mostly seen as lightweight intellectuals who were doing something that was not serious scholarly, intellectual, or even activist work. But if we think of the connection between popular culture, the state, and the public (as discussed by Chomsky) and add to that the ubiquitous nature of popular culture, and the commodification and consumerism it engenders, we should definitely take it and those studying it seriously.

I focus on gender and race because, to me, those are the two markers that are exploited the most in popular culture. And I mean exploited in the broad sense, that is, these two markers are the ones that have been used, (re)constructed, (re)presented, coded, and commodified the most.

Some may argue that social class is exploited as much as these two markers (if not more), but to me social class plays a different role in popular culture. I see social class not as another category exploited by popular culture, but as the "primer" upon which any other category is "painted." In fact, social class (especially the pervasive representation of the U.S. middle class in popular culture as the only legitimate social standing) is a good tool for analyzing the connection between popular culture and capitalism, for popular culture is

110

constantly and consistently selling us the same image: that of a happy, and more importantly "normal" middle class status. Thus, more than a social marker, social class is the basis of popular culture, a basis that is always forceful, but sometimes invisible. By way of being omnipresent, and being a constant, (middle) social class in popular culture is taken for granted. Race and gender, however, are a different story, for they operate as tellers of otherness. And, these traces of "otherness" are reflective of the particular time in which they were created. For instance, we can trace changes in portrayals of women, men, whites, and folks of color in popular culture, not to mention the more complicated portrayal of intersecting makers – for example, women of color in every television show.

What is really fascinating to me is the fact that we can test any ideas we have about race or gender relations on any medium of popular culture. For instance, you can see Eduardo Bonilla-Silva's thesis of a post-civil rights racism portrayed on television in every contemporary reality show. David Leonard and I wrote an article on the third season of *American Idol*, and we are able to explain the majority of the racial dynamics that unfolded using Bonilla-Silva. And of course, Bonilla Silva did not develop his theory from reality television. What this suggests to me is (and this is not necessarily a new insight) that, as a (re)creation of the broader society, television in particular and popular culture more generally reflect the social dynamics of their time.

In perhaps one of the most cleverly named chapters of all time, "Better than Crest: Consequences of the Selective Whitening and Mainstreaming of Latinos in the U.S. (The Case of Popular Culture)," you deal with some hot button issues. Why did you think it was important to write this

piece and what do you feel are your most important points?

"Better than Crest" was my way of trying to understand the increasing phenomenon that Latinos have become in U.S. popular culture since the 1990s at the same time that I was trying to make others understand that regardless of how much money JLo is making a year, for instance, the majority of Latinos/Latinas in the United States still find themselves in a precarious position vis-à-vis the economy and their treatment in society. More to the point, the article was a response to my students, many of whom kept insisting that things are okay now for Latinos because mainstream society is now employing hordes of Latinos (as one of my students put it) in films and television. Thus, I decided to address the Latino phenomenon in U.S. popular culture as an answer to those kinds of comments.

In the article, I argue that Latinos are being "tracked" by mainstream society in three different ways. Mainly, they are being (1) mainstreamed in brown (I use Jennifer López to illustrate this position – Eva Longoria is the perfect example these days) where Latinos in this category are "allowed and encouraged to be brown" by mainstream culture because they are perceived as non-threatening (this is especially true of many Latina women) (2) mainstreamed in white (I use Ricky Martin, Martin Sheen, and Cameron Díaz to illustrate this point) where these Latinos are regarded as "white" (either they are honorary whites – Ricky Martin, or they are just not seen as Latinos but as white – Cameron Díaz) and (3) marginalized as an ambiguous other (Rosie Pérez serves to illustrate this point) where popular culture does not quite know what to do with these Latinos, because they do not fit neat "white" or "brown" categories. In the case of Pérez, she

112

"looks" more African American than she does "Latina," and she has paid the price for that.

The bottom line is, for mainstream America, not all Latinos are created equal. And, how a Latino/a artist/entertainer is regarded by mainstream culture plays a decisive role in how that Latino/a fairs in relation to other artists/entertainers. But the most important point is that regardless of how mainstream culture regards Latino/a entertainers, the "regular" Latinos/as still have to contend with inadequate housing, education, wages, and general standards of living.

You have also written about Madonna. Why is she important to you, to Latinas, to Puerto Ricans?

Ah, the Madonna question. Some time ago, I participated in a panel with other authors who published articles about women for *Frontiers* (where the Madonna article was published). The panel was intended as a way for the authors to revisit these pieces, which (as in my case) were written a number of years ago. The interesting thing about my article on Madonna is that I wrote it when I was a (young) graduate student. If you read it, in spite of some critical elements here and there, the article is a shameless tribute to the entertainer. In the article, I celebrate Madonna, the entertainer and the woman, for giving me a different perspective of what a woman ought to be. This, of course, was in the 1980s, when Madonna was big, and I was an impressionable adolescent trying to come to terms with the daily "drag" of being a girl in a patriarchal and highly Catholic country. I even finished the article with something about Madonna being a symbol of women's empowerment. Needless to say, if I were to write that article today, it would have a different tone (though again, I guess I could say the same about most of my published works). To be honest, I would not take back what I said about Madonna in

113

that article, but if I were to write it today, I would be a lot more critical than I was, because in the end, Madonna was an enterprise and an enterprise should never be(come) a symbol of empowerment. But I did not know that when I was thirteen, which is why I am not taking it back. Insofar as the article was a personal account based on my experiences, it should stand as a testament to those experiences. On a broader level, the account also serves as an example of the ways in which popular culture can and does serve as a tool of empire. That is to say, Madonna came to us (Puerto Rican girls) courtesy of the colonial relationship between Puerto Rico and the United States, and positive or negative, the infiltration of popular culture by way of empire should be documented.

Tell us more about the negatives of Madonna.

Madonna was a woman; a woman making her way through a troubled world and an even more troubled arena – Hollywood. However, she was also a tool of empire, and she was an empire herself, something I did not realize when I was a kid. For me, she was "it," and I never questioned her role in my development as a passive consumer of goods and ideologies. At the same time that I was gaining new understandings about women's roles in society, I was also gaining understanding and developing an affinity with American culture (including the ideals of individualism, America as a land of opportunity, etc). Something I did not realize as an adolescent was that whatever sense of entitlement we gained (girls in Puerto Rico and the U.S.) by way of Madonna, it translated into personal (material) profit for the artist. It also turned into material profit for the U.S.

Another important aspect to consider here is that, in a weird way, Madonna also appropriated aspects of our culture (she had a kind of fetish for Latinos and Latino cultures), which in retrospect made the whole Madonna thing that many Puerto

114

Rican girls experienced a little twisted (we idolized her and she turned us, our men, and our culture into fetishes). Frances Negrón-Muntaner has a really good take on this aspect of Madonna in her book *Boricua Pop* when she says: "Arriving in New York City in 1978, Madonna quickly came to see Boricuas and other Latinos as raw sources of sexual and cultural energy to be enjoyed, plundered, and eventually drawn from to reproduce." Thus not only did she gain from our "revolution," but as a representative of the U.S. empire, she took things away from us, without any contemplation of what that meant.

So what's wrong with children's films? You have written on Disney, Pixar, and Dreamworks productions.

Children's films can be incredibly deceiving, for we dismiss them as just that: movies for children. Mary Bloodsworth-Lugo, Richard King, and I argue that these films ought to actually be taken seriously because they serve as important agents of socialization for children. If you pay close attention to them, beyond the fantastic computer-generated images and special effects, you can see how these films offer viewers (children and adults as well) suspiciously familiar lessons. They are a sort of audio-visual reinforcement of cultural ideologies (involving gender roles, race, social class, the importance of conquering one's fears, and the rewards of hard work, to name a few). Those lessons are what make the stories in these films powerful agents of socialization. I like Elizabeth Freeman's idea of children's films as "portable professors." I also like Henry Giroux's explanation that animated films for children, along with the corporations that produce them – Disney, Pixar, and Dreamworks – are "regulating culture," and thus profoundly influencing the daily lives of children.

115

In addition to film, television has drawn your critical eye. Let's talk about one of your favorite shows *American Idol*.

Yes, I guess I must confess that for me, watching American Idol is one of the (not so few) indulgences I allow myself. However, indulgence notwithstanding, I watch this show (much like I watch any other television show) with a critical lens. Thus, it is hard not to see events unfolding in the show in a similar vein as I see them unfolding in other venues: with racial and gender connotations. As I mentioned, David Leonard and I wrote a piece on the third season of the show. Race, racism, and gender were present from the start. We begin our discussion with the racial and racist connotations of the public's reaction to William Hung's audition, and we finish the article with an analysis of the racial and racist connotations of the reactions to Fantasia Barrino, the season's winner. This goes back to what I was saying about popular culture reflecting society's views at the time. In this case, we have a show that is teaching us about gender and race relations in twenty-first century America.

You and David Leonard have also been working on Latinos and Latinas in the *United States: An Encyclopedia of History, Society, and Culture*. Why did you begin this project?

This project emerged from what we saw as a need to understand that Latinos in the U.S. do not operate in a vacuum. We are seeking to provide a most comprehensive (as comprehensive as it is possible with this kind of project) catalogue of names, places, and events that connect Latinos to the U.S. (that says Latinos are part of the U.S.) while simultaneously establishing distinct patterns of experiencing the U.S. and living (as interlocking cultures) in the U.S. Also, we felt there was a need for a project of this magnitude that

116

would reach beyond the halls of academia. Though it can certainly be used by undergraduates, with this project, we are trying to reach high school students, so they can learn about events and people in Latino history that are not necessarily included in their curriculum.

What was toughest about assembling this encyclopedia?

The encyclopedia was an incredibly taxing project – time-consuming and tedious throughout, but nothing compared with the decisions David and I had to make at the start, when we began organizing the entries. We agonized over terminology specifically, over the term "Hispanics." Should we use this term? Should we allow contributors to use it if that's the term with which they feel most comfortable? Should we use it for specific purposes (for instance, when citing governmental documents using the term, etc.)? Because of its origin, implications, and history, David and I do not use the term (it really makes me cringe when I hear it, actually), but we did not want to leave people out, and we debated about imposing our views about terminology on our contributors. We finally decided not to tell contributors what term to use (or not to use) and decided to deal with the situation on a case-to-case basis.

PETER C. ROLLINS

Professor Peter C. Rollins is Regents Professor at Oklahoma State University and received the Oklahoma Humanities Award. He was associate editor of the *Journal of Popular Culture* and the *Journal of American Culture*, first Vice-President then President for the Popular Culture Association, and Director of Development for the Popular Culture Association/American Culture Association.

He has published myriad articles and books, including *America Reflected* (New Academia Publishing, 2010); *Hollywood's Indian* (The University Press of Kentucky, 2003) edited with John E. O'Connor; and *Hollywood as Historian* (The University of Kentucky Press, 1997).

In addition to being a prolific writer, Professor Rollins has also made many films, including a three part series *Television's Vietnam* and *Will Rogers' 1920s: A Cowboy's Guide to the Times* which won first place at the Oklahoma Film Festival, the Bronze Medallion at the Himisfilm International Film Festival, the Bronze Hugo at the Chicago Film Festival, the Chris Award at the Columbus Film Festival, and the CINE Golden Eagle.

Currently, Professor Rollins continues his activities with the Film and History League, and he is one of the editors for the league's journal, *Film and History*.

When you were an undergraduate, you transferred from Dartmouth to Harvard. Tell us about that decision.

My family has attended Dartmouth College since the early

years of the nineteenth century. Initially, the Rollins clan came from New Hampshire and Dartmouth was not too far away. The next stop for the college-bound Rollins men was Harvard Law School where they prepared to be future Daniel Websters. The lovely H.H. Richardson-designed chapel on the Dartmouth campus in Hanover, New Hampshire, is the Rollins Chapel. In the 1920s, when my grandfather, Daniel A. Rollins, drove his Cadillac North from Brookline, Massachusetts, to Hanover, he would stop the automobile at a critical point near the school and say to his family: "Now we are on the sacred soil of Dartmouth College." That reverence was passed on to us with great solemnity.

I grew up singing Dartmouth songs and visiting the Hanover campus for football games during the fall season. My brother, Philip, was a lead fullback on the football team, so we had special reason for attending the games during that glorious season in New England. There was no other choice for me, and Dartmouth was most agreeable, accepting me in the spring of my junior year in high school under an "early admissions" program.

I loved the courses offered and I loved the library. My music appreciation courses were particularly informative as was my experience of singing in the Rollins Chapel Choir. Unfortunately, the all-male atmosphere at the school fostered a locker room atmosphere: I have nothing against locker room discussions and language, but I do have objections to that style carrying over into every other aspect of campus life – discussions in class, arguments in the dormitories, even essays written in slang and accepted by professors. On one occasion, I received a paper back from an anonymous grader in Dartmouth's "Independent Reading Program" in which I was told to "take pipe." This comment reflected an anti-intellectual dimension to campus life – it was not the entire

119

atmosphere, but it used up a lot of oxygen.

The fraternity system was irritating. I remember visiting a leading fraternity and picking up a freshman directory. Each freshman's entry had markings by members of the group; one, in particular, really disturbed me. A particularly brilliant freshman from Chicago had the following written over his face: "a shit head." This was a young man who was a concert pianist, delightful humorist, and brilliant student. I was repelled.

Finally, the English Department at Dartmouth at the time was deeply into a New Criticism approach to literature, and a number of the professors were fans of the Southern Agrarians. Literature was studied for its Freudian technical literary devices and Freudian symbols while the historical contexts for literature were neglected. Looking back on the history of American literary criticism, I can now understand that the department was partly a broad reaction against the work of V.L. Parrington and others who emphasized context over the content of literature. The reaction makes sense retrospectively, but did not make sense to me at the time.

In the meantime, I met a high school classmate – who is now a Princeton professor of philosophy – who was enrolled in an honors program at Harvard, a program called History and Literature. This program combined literature classes with history and fine arts. Mark was enthusiastic about the program, and he certainly made a life-changing impression on me. At the end of the sophomore year, I applied to Harvard (and the History and Literature program) as a junior and was accepted in that status without having to repeat or add classes.

History and Literature was a program devised by Barrett

120

Wendell (1855-1921) to foster an interdisciplinary study of literature, a real breakthrough at the time; indeed, the study of American literature was quite an innovation as was Wendell's ground-breaking book, *American Literature* (1900). Over time, the honors program had been subdivided into British, American, and European components and was a tutorial offering for the last two years of college – with a comprehensive examination at the end of the junior year to qualify for the senior experience and senior essay. (Like others, mine is in the Widener Library catalog for the world to inspect; it was quite controversial at the time and caused quite a tempest in the Film & History teapot.)

My first tutor was Michael Weinberg, and in our first meeting he told me he was putting me on an intensive program for the comprehensives. I would take my classes in addition to the tutorial, but would read 1000 pages per week for the tutorial – although there were sometimes overlaps. Off we went through the Puritans, the Jacksonians, the Social Darwinians, the Populists, and, on the literary side, the Captivity Narratives, the satires of the Connecticut Wits, the Federalist Papers, the great Romantics, etc. It was an exciting and strenuous program enhanced by the famous Harvard "Reading Period" during which a serious student could really turn out substantive papers based on real research and thought. Along the way, a few of my essays were read to sophomore classes as objects for emulation, and I wrote a few articles for a newspaper on another campus – where another high school friend was the literary editor. My *nom de plume* was "Smelfungus," the moniker bestowed upon Smollet by Sterne – which I had encountered as the *nom de plume* of Alan Heimert, the scholar who would become my mentor. In any case, I was enormously busy and enormously happy with this challenging life of the mind although, concurrently, I was a member of the rugby team.

121

For me, the move from Dartmouth College to Harvard University had been a wonderful and liberating experience. My father was very disappointed with me and declined to speak to me for months thereafter, although he did pay the bills without complaint. Looking back, I admire his attitude; when I asked about applying for scholarships, he told me that other people needed such support more than I did, and they should have the opportunity to avail themselves of it. Good for Dad.

After you graduated, you were commissioned a lieutenant in the Marines and did a tour of duty in Vietnam. Talk to us about that experience and how it affected you professionally.

While an undergraduate, we were expected to be ready for the draft or to join an ROTC program of some sort to prepare for military service in the officer corps. Many chose the various options, but the Marine Corps Platoon Leader Class was very attractive to me because it demanded summer service and freed the officer candidates to be academics during the school year – no military science classes, no drills, etc. Furthermore, my father, Daniel G. Rollins, Sr. had been a Marine Officer in World War II while my oldest brother, Daniel G. Rollins, Jr. had been in the Marines during the Korean conflict. They had both been proud of their service and that was a tradition worth pursuing. In April of my senior year in college, I turned twenty-one; upon graduating in June, I was sworn in as a Marine officer by my father – who was a notary public and could administer oaths. The ceremony was serendipitously located within twenty-five yards of the site of the Boston Tea Party. Dad pinned on my Lieutenant's bars to the shoulders of my white dress uniform, and we went out to lunch at the most expensive restaurant in Boston.

122

During previous summers – of 1960 and then of 1962 – I had attended six-week sessions of officer "boot camp" in Quantico, Virginia. The officer system stressed physical endurance and strength more than drill and discipline – although we had plenty of the latter. Long marches along the rolling fire breaks of Virginia were true tests of physical readiness, especially in the foetid atmosphere of Virginia in summer. Young men allergic to bees learned about them in the lush woods and lay on the side of the trail as we hurried by, trying not to lose interval. Those with an intolerance for heat collapsed on the trail and had to be carried in litters to awaiting trucks; in some cases, serious victims of heat stroke were tossed into plastic tubs of ice water to force their temperatures down. One particularly grueling march saw 180 members of the company depart from Camp Upsher and no more than sixty-five return on foot. As one of those who returned, it was hard not to take pride in surviving this ultimate Marine Corps test of strength, tenacity, and will. Our drill sergeants seldom used physical intimidation, but that option was always available and, sometimes, was employed. It was the atmosphere of the locker room, alas, but the atmosphere was appropriate for the mission since we were being trained to endure more hardship than ordinary people and to function as leaders even under the worst conditions. During these summers, I qualified as a Sharpshooter with the M-1 rifle; later, I would score better with the M-14 and the .45 caliber pistol, earning Expert badges in each category. (As a left-handed shooter, I had trouble reloading the M-1 during the rapid-fire portion of the qualifications.)

Marksmanship may seem like a minor detail to civilians, but is enormously important to Marines, a real sign of excellence – for the obvious reason that it is a real challenge to go through the qualifications and achieve either the sharpshooter

123

or expert badges. Again, the goal was grace under pressure.

The Marine Corps stressed organization, leadership, and service to others. We were rewarded – by the supervisors and by our peers – for achievement and excellence. Most of us discovered that really devoting oneself to a task led to excellence in most cases. We also learned that errors on our part redounded to confusion, disillusionment, or death to others. For example, calling in the grid coordinates of the observer position rather than the position of the target can yield explosive results. Not knowing that there is a round in the chamber of your weapon can lead to irrevocable tragedy among your friends as can excessive fear in combat. The Marine Corps created an environment of intense pressure and physical challenge in the training so that anything thereafter was a cake walk. We were constantly reminded of the challenges of past generations of Marines and their sacrifices – especially by the World War II and Korean Veterans who constantly related personal anecdotes about why we should not walk along the crest of hills, etc. An atmosphere of destruction bred conscientiousness among those who sought to lead. (And I am still glad I missed "the Coldest War," that war in Korea. How many dark evenings did we practice night attacks!)

The Marines with whom I served in Vietnam have all of my admiration and respect. Unlike their cinematic representations, they were ordinary Americans who did extraordinary things for their country in a moral and intelligent way. The Marines I served with are still proud of their service to country and came back to lead in business and academe. Of course, upon returning home, they found a country confused about the values and mission of America – the beginnings of a cultural struggle that persists until this day.

124

During my service years between 1963 and 1966, I laid out a reading program for myself with the notion that I would be going back to Harvard for the History of American Civilization Program there, a graduate extension of the History and Literature Program – indeed, with many of the same professors. My project was to read about eras and to expose myself to books that I would not study in graduate school; the resulting list led me to Asian and European history; economics and philosophy; and various schools of psychology. As the proud owner of *The Great Books of the Western World*, a series very popular in the 1960s (and a replacement of *The Harvard Classics*), I went from volume to volume. Adam Smith's *The Wealth of Nations*; Karl Marx's *Capital*; Gibbon's *Decline and Fall of the Roman Empire* were on the list, and I had time to savor them for their details and, surprisingly, their literary style. I even read all kinds of good books by William James (along with Jonathan Edwards, the greatest mind America has produced) and Sigmund Freud; in later years, I have found much amusement in reading Freudian interpretations of literature and film and comparing their awkward results with the concepts of Freud himself.

In any case, the reading program paid unanticipated benefits. I took the Graduate Record Exam (GRE) in history for the afternoon session and must have done very well because I was offered NDEA Title IV fellowships by Harvard and Chicago; my application reached Berkeley too late to be considered for such largesse. Knowing the library and the professors made the Harvard choice pretty obvious to me, and the financial package combining the fellowship, teaching fees as tutor in the History and Literature Program, plus the G.I. Bill made graduate school a pretty cushy situation.

Tell us about the ideological climate at Harvard.

125

Graduate school at Harvard during the late 1960s and early 1970s was a fascinating experience. Despite what is said about "Harvard Hates America" and other aspersions, it can be said without equivocation that the professors I encountered at Harvard were actually interested and concerned about the past. They had respect for the past and tried to make us understand the difficulties of understanding the past on its own terms. For this reason, they did not try to infuse current political prejudices and ideologies into our study of the History of American Civilization. Ideologues may have existed elsewhere on campus and many certainly arrived later, but people like Perry Miller, Alan Heimert, Kenneth S. Lynn, Donald Fleming, Conrad Wright, and Joel Porte were genuinely interested in an interpretation of the past which did justice to the concerns and interests *of* the past. So often, today, the contrasting approach either projects current "methodological models" on past materials or berates the past for not being as well-informed and sophisticated as we think we are. Really serious people today are interested in theory. As one of the Harvard professors told me at an American Studies Association meeting years ago, the interest in theory "absolves them of doing research." Later, Ray Browne, Founder of the Popular Culture Association, would tell me that "theory is the hiding place for scoundrels." In any case, the generation of teachers and models available to me were not politicians or ideologues manqué, but real scholars passionately committed to the life of the mind. The role could not have been more exciting, and I have been living it ever since.

During your time in graduate school, you also attended your first meeting of the American Studies Association and Popular Culture Association. How did those early years contribute to your professional interests, your professional identity?

126

As a graduate student, I attended my first professional meeting in Toledo, Ohio. It was a biennial gathering of the American Studies Association and the focus was Popular Culture. I was excited by the event and by the experience of traveling through time and space in America on an academic mission. The papers were challenging and some of the sessions strange – due to the unwillingness of people to talk – but overall, I was impressed by the approach to popular culture exemplified by so many papers. The very next year, I discovered that some of the professors in attendance – Ray Browne, Russel Nye, Tom Towers, Marshall Fishwick – had decided to create an organization devoted to such studies; the first meeting of the Popular Culture Association was held the very next year in Toledo, and it was at this meeting that I delivered my very first popular culture paper on the television series "Victory at Sea."

At this point, I must stand aside and comment on contemporary events. While in graduate school, I lived in my hometown of Brookline, Massachusetts, and commuted three times a week to Cambridge for lectures, seminars, and tutorial sessions. Most often, I traveled by the "streetcar" system of above surface and subsurface transportation, which I had grown to love as a choir boy at Trinity Church at Copley Square during my youth. I have always felt at home on mass transit and use it whenever I can without fear and without incident – even in foreign countries where it is occasionally necessary to slap the hand of a pickpocket. In any case, on the MBTA, I had time to read the *New York Times* from cover to cover and the reports from Vietnam disturbed me greatly. They had little or no relationship with my experience there, and the work of David Halberstam was particularly disturbing. He had an axe to grind about the war, and every "news" article was shaped by his agenda. I was most disturbed by the disconnect between what I had seen and

127

experienced and what the *New York Times* and the networks were reporting – especially CBS. Fellow students often questioned me about the war and always walked away unhappy with the answers they received, answers that did not conform to the media reports they had seen and believed. The climax of this problem was reached when a Vice President of a college told me, during one of my first job interviews, "We don't want your kind around here." When questioned about his meaning, he said, "You know, baby killers. We don't want your kind around here." For the first few months after this experience, I was angry but have since understood that this misguided intellectual was really my best friend: he launched me on a study of media and popular culture that continues into the present.

My study of "Victory at Sea" became a launch pad for scholarly investigations. At the very time when I was beginning this work, a small journal entitled *Film & History* was being created by John E. O'Connor and Martin Jackson. I met these two pioneers at a New Orleans meeting of the American Historical Association where I was asked to critique an historical compilation film by a Dutch filmmaker. Their encouragement led me to further studies, and the die was cast for a lifetime of scholarly investigation into the impact of film and television on American society.

In addition, the Popular Culture Association provided a forum for my work on "Victory at Sea," on Will Rogers, and on the Vietnam War – not to mention Accuracy in Media. At various points, I served as Area Chair for Film and was responsible for the creation of the Areas on Vietnam and Accuracy in Media. Alas, I later became estranged from the Vietnam Area after four years due to its mirror reflection of the media version of the war. The historical studies were recapitulating journalistic reports – the second time, to my mind, as farce.

128

In the early 1980s, I served as President of the PCA and was the national Program Chair for the organization, especially at the Wichita meeting – where we had the greatest attendance of any gathering up to that time. Many people think that the study of popular culture translates into approval of it; quite the contrary, it is the duty of scholars to identify the deleterious impact of some examples of the popular arts and to take what I call the hygienic approach. On the other hand, there is much that is entertaining, insightful, and beautiful in the popular arts, and we are foolish to turn up our noses at these virtues of games, films, buildings, and music. We need to value both Bach and Basie, not one over the other.

During the 1970s, I founded the Southwest Popular Culture Association, and the organization has grown into an annual gathering of 700-1000 people per year. I am particularly proud to have helped to create such areas of study as Motorcycle Culture, Food and Culture, Popular Religion. While not a devotee of any of them, I applaud those who investigate the meaning of what ordinary human beings do and take pleasure from. Such studies have clearly been in the tradition of Henry Nash Smith's *Virgin Land*, John William Ward's *Jackson: Symbol for an Age*, two works which carry weight among "high culture" scholars, but should point to the need to study history and culture from the bottom up. I am eternally grateful for all that Ray Browne and others did to encourage the work of people like me and I have tried to nurture young scholars coming along in their spirit – not always successfully, but always ardently.

You have been at Oklahoma State University (OSU) for your entire career. Many academics bounce around. Obviously, you found a nice fit right away.

When I visited the Oklahoma State University campus in

129

the spring of 1972, I was responding to a call for an American Studies specialist. Clinton Keeler was the head of the department, and he wanted some interdisciplinary emphasis in the curriculum; in addition, what was called The Will Rogers Project was in need of someone with literary training to add that dimension to the effort. As it turns out, the university had been funded by the state legislature to reprint the entire writings of Will Rogers, and we did so, eventually, achieving a total of twenty-two volumes – all of them authenticated, annotated, and interpreted. This effort constituted half of the job and every day was a joy.

The Will Rogers Project taught us about middle America and its frontier heritage. Will Rogers was a brilliant man who modeled himself after Huckleberry Finn and then set out to explain a changing America to itself during the first three decades of the twentieth century, from the perspective of a rural naif. In addition to the volumes of the writings, my popular culture interests forced me to look at the films as I was reading the daily articles, weeklies, and special assignment works of the Oklahoma savant. Along the way, I produced a book about Rogers and a film which won a broad spectrum of awards – to include a CINE Golden Eagle, the highest award for a non-theatrical documentary.

Will Rogers' 1920s launched me as a maker of historical films and my *Television's Vietnam: The Real Story* (SONY, 1985) and *Television's Vietnam: The Impact of Media* (SONY, 1986) were shown on PBS and then re-run on WTBS by Ted Turner. These films gave me an opportunity to have my say about the disparity between media reports and the realities of Vietnam; many people contributed to their excellence – too many to mention here.

Department heads at OSU were very supportive in my

130

projects, and I am ever grateful for the faith shown in my work by Clinton Keeler, Gordon Weaver, Jack Crane, Jack Campbell, Edward Walkiewicz, Jeffrey Walker, and Carol Moder. I am not sure what it means, but I should point out that my oldest brother, Dan, worked for the FAA as an electrical engineer for over thirty years and my brother, Philip, the Dartmouth fullback, served as an elected official in Massachusetts for over thirty years. It looks as though there is a reluctance in my family to play the market – hopefully because we have been doing our best to excel where we were.

In 1989, you earned a Regents Professorship at OSU – the first the English department ever had.

This topic is hard to address from "inside" the role. Jack Crane proposed this honorific designation to the personnel committee, and it passed the recommendation along up the chain. The Regents Professorship is reconsidered every three years, and I have earned the confidence of the university each time. Unlike other schools, OSU does not include a salary increment or special travel assistance to its Regents Professors in the humanities; we are asked to bask in the honorific glory of the role itself.

You were Associate Editor of the *Journal of Popular Culture* and the *Journal of American Culture* and succeeded John O'Connor as Editor-in-Chief of *Film & History: An Interdisciplinary Journal of Film and Television Studies*. What have you learned and what have you contributed through your experiences as an editor?

Ray Browne founded *The Journal of Popular Culture* and the *Journal of American Culture* to provide outlets for scholarship in these two areas of study and these journals have flourished over the years under Ray's leadership and the

131

daily contributions of Mrs. Pat Browne. It was my pleasure to work with them on these projects in the capacity as Associate Editor and as someone who tried to diversify the book review writing to as many members as possible.

Most of my time in the last seven years has been devoted to editing *Film & History: An Interdisciplinary Journal of Film and Television Studies* at www.filmandhistory.org. Founded by John O'Connor and Martin Jackson, this publication was the very first to take an interest in my media writing and the reinforcement had the predictable effect of encouraging me to go forward in the field. John O'Connor set a good example by organizing seminars at the Museum of Modern Art (with Dan Leab) and mounting panels at the annual meetings of the American Historical Association. John edited collections of essays by people who participated in such events and turned out two pioneering books entitled *American History/American Film* and *American History/American Television*. John was – and is – a great friend who loved to fish, to have a beer on occasion, and to tell stories about the many filmmakers he had met in his capacity as editor; in addition, he was always willing to share his experiences in the joy of scholarship.

My goal was to emulate John's qualities and activities in my capacity as Editor-in-Chief for *Film & History*. We have had panels at the AHA meetings – some covered by C-SPAN, to include sessions with film critic Michael Medved, cultural analyst Garry Wills, and filmmaker Ken Burns. (After awhile, I developed an outfit for C-SPAN appearances, a dark jacket and trouser combination humorously dubbed "the C-SPAN suit.") In any case, our sessions attracted much attention. At the NYC meeting of AHA a few years back, we organized a panel discussing Oliver Stone's *Nixon*; the panel included Oliver Stone, George McGovern, and Arthur Schlesinger, Jr. Some 1200 people attended this televised event, and a second ballroom was opened up with sound piped in from the session. In these events, *Film & History* was ably assisted by Robert Toplin, a member of the Editorial Board and a leading scholar in the field. In 2000, we conducted our own conference in California with the topic of "The American Presidency in Film, TV, and History"; the event was well attended and spawned two major anthologies edited by me and O'Connor: *The West Wing: The American Presidency as Television Drama* and a second effort on a broader topic, *Hollywood's White House: The American Presidency in Film and History*. In the fall of 2002, we conducted our second biennial conference in Kansas City with the topic of "The American West(s) in Film, TV, and History." This conference produced a year's worth of articles for the journal and shaped a book.

What I have discovered as an editor have been the following lessons: not enough people subscribe to journals and, if they subscribe, they often do not read them; scholars should demand the same attention to detail and word choice that they ask of their students; it is often the case that a novice in the field will do a better job – and in a more reasonable time frame – than a leading scholar. Most of these lessons are negative. On the positive side, it is delightful to deal with people who are excited about what they do, and it is a joy to see a publication result that reflects the work of the scholars, the editor, the associate editor, and the printer. When everyone is working together, there is cumulative value to the result. What I have discovered for myself is that long hours of work can be rewarding and a positive experience if they are for a good cause; in addition, it is great to see a job come to a fruitful conclusion with each word hitting the proverbial target. There must be some link back to the Marine Corps experience: people working as a team can accomplish great results; concentration and dedication to achieving a mission can overcome the lethargy and indifference that characterize

133

much of the world. Finally, we need to follow the example of good leaders and we also need to set a good example for others; we need to learn how to be mentored and then to mentor others when our time arrives to carry out that role.

There is a humorous anecdote to explain the joys of this activity. Back in 1989, we came out with *Hollywood as Historian*. One of the essayists wrote at least eight drafts of his article; by the time it was accepted, he would not talk to me and was, apparently, an enemy for life. A year or so later and then, again, after five years, he admitted that he had never written anything which had received so much attention and praise. The praise rightfully goes to him for the wisdom and research, but there was a crowded tension with the editor that brought the best out of him. I treasure the memory of the swing back this way and hope that it will be true for the recent contributors to the journal and to our anthologies.

Unlike most academics who only write books, you have made seven historical films: *Film as Art: Frank Capra and the Art of Editing (1996)*; *The Great Victory of World War II: Oklahoma's Veterans Remember (1995)*; *Television's Vietnam: The Battle of Khe Sanh (1992)*; *Dignity and Dependence: New Ways of Escaping from Poverty (1987)*; *Television's Vietnam: The Impact of Media (1985)*; *Television's Vietnam: The Real Story (1984)*; *Will Rogers' 1920s: A Cowbo''s Guide to the Times (1976)*. Why did you decide to go into filmmaking?

When I was just jumping into film and history scholarship, I attended an AHA meeting in New York City where John O'Connor and Martin Jackson (here they are, again) were chairing a *Film & History* session on "The Historian as Filmmaker" with Patrick Griffin as the speaker. Griffin and Richard Raack had produced a rough cut of a compilation film entitled *Goodbye Billy: America Goes to War, 1917-1918*, a wonderful and suggestive experiment in which the historians involved actually *made* the film and employed film language to get their message across. The basic thrust of the presentation was that historians should stop relying on audiovisualists to make historical productions because the typical filmmaker does not have the feel for the archival materials or the respect for facts – as opposed to impact – which is part of the training of academics. Later, in essays for *The History Teacher* and *Film & History*, Griffin and Raack spelled out an aesthetic and a methodology for filmmaking by students of culture. These principles have not received the attention they deserve.

It would be difficult for me to have been more impressed by what I heard. At the end of the session, I went up and introduced myself to the organizers and to the speaker. Griffin, in a model for mentors, communicated with me about his project, his goals for filmmaking, and mailed me extensive bibliographical hints and copies of his work. He really set me on a course toward writing essays with a cinematic pen. Once at Oklahoma State University and immersed in the extensive documents of image and sound related to Will Rogers, I asked Griffin and Raack to work with me on a film about the Oklahoma satirist. They agreed and, with the help of the National Endowment for the Humanities and released time from Oklahoma State, I was on my way. The resulting film, *Will Rogers' 1920s* purposely restricted itself to the early period of Rogers' work – with the idea of picking up the Great Depression role in a sequel. Using recordings from the Will Rogers Memorial, along with still materials, as well as interviews with members of his family and those who worked with him in Hollywood, we created a historical compilation film which won a CINE Golden Eagle, as well as a number of lesser awards – all of them valued, of course. The film sold widely and we paid back to the NEH every penny it provided for us to make it. We also purchased audiovisual materials for the university with the remaining profits.

The work with Griffin and Raack set me on the filmmaking course, and I have been lucky enough to make subsequent projects. During the academic year of 1977, I spent two semesters at the National Humanities Institute at Yale University, an NEH-funded operation under the supervision of a renaissance man, the famous Maynard Mack. Mack had a record that was marked by a passion to share Shakespeare with ordinary people, to include high school audiences. To this end, he had made films that I had used in my classes; his compilation on *Hamlet* is particularly valuable and featured the Yale University Players to illustrate key points made in the presentation. One of Mack's goals was to encourage humanists to use media; in addition, he urged us to bring our message to audiences around New England. As part of the NHI program, I gave multiple presentations in Maine, Massachusetts, New York City, and Connecticut as well as at national meetings of PCA/ACA. In part as a reward for a good-faith effort, Mack promised to help us obtain funding for a project I had in mind: a study of the Tet offensive of 1968 as a test case for media misreporting during the Vietnam war.

David Culbert of Louisiana State U and C. Townsend Ludington, III ("Lud"), were involved in the research and interview process. Ludington found a way to fund an ambitious conference on the Tet Offensive at the University of North Carolina. Despite an unseasonable spring snow storm, leading journalists (Peter Braestrup, Charles Mohr), military and diplomatic figures (General C. Westmoreland, Douglas Pike), and television producers (Robert Northshield of NBC) along with eminent scholars on the subject (among

136

them Lawrence Lichty) attended this meeting where panels and talks were conducted; after major sessions, Culbert and I interviewed the participants, getting the essence of their message on film with the help of a hard-working film crew from OSU. With funding from the Rockefeller Foundation, we went on to purchase large quantities of footage from the U.S. Marine Corps and the National Archives. We conducted further interviews and had camera coverage of combat art by Marines, subjective records of life in the combat zone preserved in the U.S. Marine Corps Museum in Washington, DC. A year later, Culbert traveled to Tulsa, Oklahoma, where we rented a news studio, and he served as an excellent on-camera narrator for the film with an urban skyline behind him as we used the devices of television news to critique television news. When completed, the film was entitled *Television's Vietnam: The Impact of Visual Images* (1983) and lasted a "short" two and a half hours. The goal of the film was to compare/contrast news reports from Vietnam with memories of soldiers, marines, and diplomats. For me, it was an opportunity to critique the misleading reports of the 1960s and 1970s while paying homage to the fine Marines who served their country and its flag.

Not much attention was paid to our production until a copy was rented from the OSU AV Center by someone who pirated a copy and sent it to Reed Irvine at Accuracy in Media in Washington, DC. Irvine and his staff, especially Bernie Yoh, loved the production and shared their enthusiasm with me. Concurrently, PBS (through WGBH, Boston) had produced a thirteen-part series entitled *Vietnam: A Television History* (1983), and this series had stirred up phone calls from veterans and émigrés angry about the distortions of the series – especially the white washing of Communist leaders such as Ho Chi Minh and the denigration of the American fighting man. Many who called Irvine (correctly) predicted that the

137

series would be purchased by school systems after the broadcast run; indeed, the series had three broadcasts (i.e. thirteen programs shown three times) and then became very popular in the classroom. During the very first call, I told Irvine that what was needed was a two-part series: the first show would be devoted to a comparison/contrast of the series with the historical truth of experienced people from Vietnam; the second show could get into the issues addressed by my two and a half hour work. In preparation for the effort, AIM announced a two-day conference at a downtown Washington hotel and started to search for funding.

The conference, like the one organized by Townsend Ludington ("Lud") for the earlier project, brought to our door diplomats, boat people, veterans, and government figures. After public sessions, these figures came upstairs to our cameras and shared their views in more personalized interviews. Afterward, I traveled to various points of the nation to collect needed archival materials. In a generous offer, the President of ABC gave us free access (costs only) to his archive, a major contribution to our efforts. (He had given PBS access on the same basis and felt duty-bound to do the same for us.) The resulting programs, each an hour in length, became very controversial even in the production stage; for example, when the Chairman of the NEH gave us $35,000 from his discretionary fund, and then PBS offered to show the programs, a number of television critics took umbrage and attacked Bruce Christensen, President of PBS, for "caving in to political pressure." Until muzzled by the President of WGBH, the producer of the PBS series did everything possible to feed these fires of discontent. In 1985, the first program, entitled *Television's Vietnam: The Real Story*, was aired and received a lot of critical attention. Tom Shales of the *Washington Post* had little good to say about the show, but the *New York Times* review by John Corry was quite positive. In

1986, *Television's Vietnam: The Impact of Media* aired and later was picked up by Ted Turner for WTBS where it was broadcast on three occasions. That our on-camera narrator was Charlton Heston attracted further attention to the programs; he was a joy to work with and, like a true professional, was very solicitous to my goals as the director of the programs. (He often asked me to call him "Chuck," to which I answered, "You bet, Mr. Heston.") Both programs were picked up by Sony Video and Blockbuster Video was given an exclusive sales agreement. A number of articles have been written by me on the production and reception of these programs and can be found in my *Vietnam in Popular Culture*, a collection of my scholarly work on Vietnam, but also a source for the scripts of both programs.

Unless something dramatic happens in the next few years, the Vietnam programs will stand as my most important work as a filmmaker. It would be hard for me to over-stress the joy in having delivered my message in such a way to so many people and with all of the right production values. Anyone using the PBS series in the classroom should introduce our programs for discussion purposes. There are even essays available on how to do so, including a thoughtful one by Tom Slater in chapter fourteen of *Inventing Vietnam: The War in Film and Television*.

Not only are you very productive in your research life, you have also been known as an excellent teacher and mentor. Tell us about your relationship with your students.

I do not like to hear people talk about their teaching skills; the information is always self-serving.

It is always my goal to improve the language sensitivities of undergraduates: I require that every student show me a copy of the Webster's Collegiate Dictionary (eleventh edition) or an equivalent; every class in film begins with training in film language. Students are urged to rewrite exams for two extra points, etc.

I have had good graduate students and "bad" graduate students. My most important goal has been to get them to professional meetings, get them published, and – as a result – get them jobs. We have an excellent track record in the employment stage; after they obtain their first job, they must build a career. I will help them, but they must be diligent and productive and deserve the collegial support.

Some scholars are still skeptical about the study of American popular culture as a serious discipline. Why do you think that is so and why would you disagree?

From the earliest days of study in the History and Literature program at Harvard University, I was told that I should be interested in both "high culture" and "low culture." I internalized that lesson in 1961 and have been guided by it ever since. For reasons having to do with an inherent snobbery by some academics, there is the false belief that the study of popular culture is the same as an endorsement of it. While leaders like my mentor Ray Browne seem to say as much from time to time, it has always been my belief that we study culture – high or low – to understand the human spirit. As far back as Mozart, even "high culture" artists have realized the potential of popular forms and have reveled in the use of popular language, music, and folklore in their work; true scholars can do no less.

Coming close to home, I am a great believer in the virtues of such studies as Perry Miller's *The Puritan Mind* (two volumes), but one of the most exciting books in my early days

140

was J.W. Ward's *Andrew Jackson: Symbol for an Age* (1962), a study which looked at popular music, cartoons, and political rhetoric to define the meaning of a major figure in the early age of democracy. Yet A.M. Schlesinger, Jr.'s *Age of Jackson* offers another layer of insight into the times, one which includes the works of "high culture." We should tap all available sources to understand an era. My undergraduate honors essay was on Orestes Brownson, a high culture figure, and my dissertation was on Benjamin Whorf, a linguist. Incidentally, while visiting the Notre Dame University campus for a Vietnam-related conference in 1988, I had the opportunity to pray over Brownson's burial stone in the crypt chapel of the immense basilica.

I have nothing against high culture and am pretty much a cultural snob in my private tastes. This element stems, in part, from singing professionally in the Trinity Church choir for four years as a child while attending the Boston Symphony regularly with my father who, although a lawyer, had aspired to be a composer in the impressionist style and to study style with Nadia Boulanger in Paris. (The Great Depression got in the way.) These are personal prejudices and choices that I can easily separate from my studies as a scholar interested in American culture – with particular interest in media and the impact of film and television on history.

What projects are you working on right now?

I am not in the best health. My left hip was replaced. I experienced a heart attack and have changed my lifestyle, to include my work habits. I exercise for forty-five to sixty minutes per day, sleep for one hour each day, and try to make up the lost time by working into the evening. Of course, I worked all day prior to these catastrophes, but have decided to become my own project – sort of like the challenge at the rifle

141

range in the Marine Corps. I find consolation and peace in my religious faith – a faith rekindled by a wonderful Episcopal church out here in the Keystone Lake area just west of Tulsa. My study overlooks eight miles of lake; during the winter months, eagles glide by along the shore in search of prey.

While I thought I was dying in the Stillwater Medical Center, I made a list of priorities for the future. At the top of the list were our cat and Susan Rollins, my very special wife. Down the list was *Film & History* and Film and History League events. I drew a line and chose to drop all below the line – which meant the PCA/ACA activities and editorial tasks, leadership roles in veterans organizations, and various editorial boards and honorific titles. These moves may be selfish, but they are prudent, and I have assumed the role of "Mr. Moderation" and remind people daily about the various activities not permitted to the new, Moderate Me.